China's Ambassadors of Christ to the Nations

Evangelical Missiological Society Monograph Series

Anthony Casey, Allen Yeh, Mark Kreitzer, and Edward L. Smither
SERIES EDITORS

A Project of the Evangelical Missiological Society
www.emsweb.org

China's Ambassadors of Christ to the Nations

A Groundbreaking Survey

Tabor Laughlin

☙PICKWICK *Publications* • Eugene, Oregon

CHINA'S AMBASSADORS OF CHRIST TO THE NATIONS
A Groundbreaking Survey

Evangelical Missiological Society Monograph Series 6

Copyright © 2020 Tabor Laughlin. All rights reserved. Except for brief quotations in critical publications or reviews, no part of this book may be reproduced in any manner without prior written permission from the publisher. Write: Permissions, Wipf and Stock Publishers, 199 W. 8th Ave., Suite 3, Eugene, OR 97401.

Pickwick Publications
An Imprint of Wipf and Stock Publishers
199 W. 8th Ave., Suite 3
Eugene, OR 97401

www.wipfandstock.com

PAPERBACK ISBN: 978-1-7252-5796-2
HARDCOVER ISBN: 978-1-7252-5797-9
EBOOK ISBN: 978-1-7252-5798-6

Cataloguing-in-Publication data:

Names: Laughlin, Tabor, author.

Title: China's ambassadors of christ to the nations : a groundbreaking survey / by Tabor Laughlin.

Description: Eugene, OR: Pickwick Publications, 2020. | Evangelical Missiological Society Monograph Series 6. | Includes bibliographical references.

Identifiers: ISBN 978-1-7252-5796-2 (paperback) | ISBN 978-1-7252-5797-9 (hardcover) | ISBN 978-1-7252-5798-6 (ebook)

Subjects: LCSH: Missions—China | China—Religion | Christianity and culture—China.

Classification: BR1288 L38 2020 (print) | BR1288 (ebook)

Manufactured in the U.S.A.   03/20/20

Contents

List of Tables | vii
Acknowledgments | ix

1. **Introduction** | 1
   Context for the Problem   1
   Research Problem and Research Questions   10
   Significance of the Research and Anticipated New Contribution   11
   Theoretical Construct and Definition of Terms   12
   Limitations and Delimitations   13
   Structure   14

2. **Precedent Literature** | 15
   Effectively Building Relationships Cross-Culturally   15
   Missionary Attrition   33
   Missionary Training   40
   Church in China   43
   The Contribution of this Study   45

3. **Research Methodology** | 47
   Informant Selection, Sampling Criteria, and Sampling Procedure   48
   Instrumentation, Data Collection, Recording Procedures, Transcribing, and Data Analysis   51
   Validity, Reliability, Possible Biases, and Permissions   55

CONTENTS

4. Presentation of Findings | 57
   Cross-Cultural Adjustment and Coping   62
   Pre-Field Preparation   71
   Cross-Cultural Relationships   80
   Host Language Ability   87
   Level of Comfort on the Field   89
   Factors for Staying on the Field   92
   Other Positive or Negative Experiences to Share   102

5. Analysis of Findings | 105
   Research Questions   105
   Emerging Themes   106
   Implications   126

6. Conclusion and Recommendations | 138

Appendix A: Interview Protocol | 143
Appendix B: Informed Consent Letter | 146
Appendix C: Initial Email Correspondence with Missionaries | 148
Appendix D: Initial Email Correspondence with Missionary Contacts | 149
Bibliography | 151

Tables

4.1. Interviewees' Background Information | 58

4.2. Interviewees' Missionary Preparation | 72

4.3. Most Helpful Pre-Field Preparation They Received | 76

4.4. Pre-Field Preparation They Wish They Had Received, but Did Not | 80

Acknowledgments

I CAN GIVE THANKS for help from the Intercultural Studies faculty at Trinity International University. All of my faculty have helped me at Trinity Evangelical Divinity School, particularly Craig Ott, Harold Netland, Robert Priest, Tite Tienou, Alice Ott, Darrell Whiteman, and Peter Cha. Dr. Ott and Dr. Netland have aided me in advising me in my dissertation. Dr. Ott in particular has helped me significantly in working on my dissertation and pushing me to make it as good as I possibly can make it.

I also need to thank my wife. She has been patient and supportive during my three years here at Trinity. She has provided lots of encouragement for persevering in the PhD. Plus she has helped me in preparing for my comprehensive exam, dissertation proposal, and dissertation defense hearings. I also thank Debbie Seckler for helping me with my dissertation. She has helped me with improving the dissertation's clarity and in putting it into better academic writing form.

I must also thank close friends at Trinity Evangelical Divinity School. They have also played a part in encouraging me towards completing my PhD. These friends and I regularly meet and are able to discuss our schoolwork and our lives. These tight friendships have helped me during times when I have felt discouraged or tired from PhD work.

1

Introduction

THE PURPOSE OF THIS monograph is to explore the experience of Chinese missionaries, factors contributing to building relationships cross-culturally, and the extent to which Chinese missionaries' experiences contribute to their retention on the mission field. The focus in this dissertation is on Chinese missionaries being sent from what is commonly referred to as "Mainland China." These missionaries are from People's Republic of China, but excluding those from Hong Kong, Taiwan, and Macau. They are not sent from Chinese churches outside China. Throughout this dissertation, "China" is used to denote Mainland China, and "Chinese" is used to refer to those from Mainland China. The aim of this study is to research Chinese missionaries serving cross-culturally internationally. These are Chinese missionaries who were sent from Chinese house churches and are ministering among non-Chinese living outside China. Though the Chinese mission movement has matured over the last ten to twenty years, it is often reported that Chinese missionaries have a high attrition rate. Many allegedly return to China within a few years after being sent out. One common reason for missionary attrition for Chinese is failure to adjust cross-culturally and establish relationships with people of the host culture.

Context for the Problem

Chinese Mission Movement Challenges

Several authors write about the recent phenomenon of an increasing number of Chinese missionaries ministering to non-Chinese outside China. Sarah Eekhoff Zylstra, in a *Christianity Today* article, explains the 2015 conference Mission China 2030 held in Hong Kong, which was attended by 850 Chinese leaders.[1] The purpose of the conference and movement is to propagate sending out 20,000 missionaries from Mainland China by the year 2030. Zylstra mentions David Ro's words that the Chinese mission movement is one of the larger emerging mission movements in the world that comes from an oppressive political setting, where Christianity is strictly controlled[2]. Xu Zhiqiu describes how the Chinese government's "One Belt One Road" campaign promotes developing infrastructure and trade in Central Asia, the Middle East, and beyond. This government campaign unintentionally assists the Chinese mission movement, as Chinese missionaries will be more readily welcomed to live and serve in these mostly-Muslim countries. In the same article, Brent Fulton, former CEO and founder of the well-respected Christian organization China Source, estimated the number of Chinese missionaries working cross-culturally as "numbering in the hundreds"[3]. Fulton's estimate does not specify if he is only referring to Chinese serving cross-culturally outside of China, or he is including also Chinese serving cross-culturally within China.

David Ro writes how many Chinese Christians previously held to "Back to Jerusalem" ideals: Chinese missionaries being the "Final Torchbearer" to complete the Great Commission[4]. Though there has been much optimism related to the Chinese mission movement, Ro writes that even with the excitement within China for the "Back to Jerusalem" movement for multiple decades, this pride and nationalistic attitude about China being the "Final Torchbearer" in the Great Commission led to failure for Chinese missionaries on the mission field, which has resulted in a humbler attitude now for Chinese missionaries and mission leaders.

Ro adds how the Chinese economy is now the largest economy in the world, which should aid Chinese missionary sending. Wealthy and educated house churches in urban areas, because of their affluence, are able to afford increasing missionary sending, so it is now unnecessary for these missionaries to receive money from abroad, as was the previous case[5]. Effective Chinese mission training of future generations of Chinese pastors and missionaries requires well-educated Chinese "professors, theologians, academics, and missiologists" to now be equipped.

1. Zylstra, "Made in China," 20.
2. Zylstra, "Made in China," 21.
3. Zylstra, "Made in China," 21.
4. Ro, "Rising Missions Movement."
5. Ro, "Rising Missions Movement."

INTRODUCTION

Thomas Lee describes the Chinese mission movement, and how poor and less educated rural pastors have mission zeal, but are unqualified for missions. On the other hand, the educated urban pastors are unwilling to move abroad to serve as missionaries, though they should be better qualified for missionary service.[6] Limitations of Chinese missions in the past have included a lack of funding, and Chinese mission and church leadership lacking perspective-broadening personal international experience.[7]

Kevin Xiyi Yao writes of the need to avoid being overly optimistic about Chinese missions; one must contemplate failures and challenges of the Chinese mission movement[8]. Despite their initial mission zeal, many Chinese missionaries have returned home after a couple of years.[9] Chinese missionaries with an ethnocentric and nationalistic attitude could have paternalistic inclinations on the mission field towards hosts.[10]

Anecdotal evidence indicates that Chinese missionaries have difficulties building relationships in cross-cultural ministry. In an interview reported in *Christianity Today*, former CEO of China Source Brent Fulton commented that most Chinese missionaries working cross-culturally quit after two years.[11] Yao mentions, "The Chinese church needs to provide missionaries with better education concerning the Bible, missiology, languages, cultures, and cross-cultural communication. Most Chinese theological schools and programs do not have significant mission study components in their curriculum."[12] Lee says, "A reason the church in China did not perform its cross-cultural mission in the past [was] cross-cultural awareness and capabilities [were] insufficient."[13] From reading a Chinese website, accessed using the Chinese search engine BaiDu, Chinese mission leaders affirm that Chinese missionaries have had cross-cultural difficulties on the mission field.[14] Young Chinese missionaries may go to the mission field only to return home within one or two years because of adjustment difficulties on the mission field. Other recent Bible school graduates, because

6. Lee, "Mission China," 29.
7. Lee, "Mission China," 36.
8. Yao, "Chinese Church," 300–301.
9. Yao, "Chinese Church," 301.
10. Yao, "Chinese Church," 302.
11. Fulton as cited in Zylstra, "Made in China," 21.
12. Yao, "Chinese Church," 301.
13. Lee, "Mission China," 36.
14. CMTC, "Back to Jesus Christ."

of an absence of cross-cultural mission training, fail on the mission field as a result of culture shock.

Missionary Attrition Problem

Missionary attrition is a relevant topic in the study of missions. Mission agencies worldwide desire to have higher retention of their missionaries and minimize the problem of attrition. "Missionary attrition" refers to missionaries permanently leaving the mission field prior to completion of their anticipated time of service. This attrition can be "unpreventable," which describes those who leave the mission field for "unavoidable" reasons, such as health problems or retirement. Missionary attrition may also be "preventable": attrition stemming from causes such as an inability to adjust on the mission field, or interpersonal disagreements on the mission field or with mission agency leadership.

As for some general background information about the challenges of missionary attrition, the most noteworthy book and research about missionary attrition has been the 1997 book *Too Valuable to Lose*, commissioned by the World Evangelical Alliance (WEA) and edited by William D. Taylor. This study commissioned by the WEA was called ReMAP, which stands for Reducing Missionary Attrition Project. Taylor, in the Introduction, defines "acceptable attrition," which is attrition reasons such as planned retirement, issues with children, a change of job, or having health problems.[15] On the other hand, "preventable attrition" pertains to a lack of financial or other support from home, issues in relationships with fellow missionaries, a "lack of call," or inadequate cross-cultural training. The task in attrition research is discovering "undesirable attrition."[16] This is defined as problems connected to the missionary's family, sending base, personal life, cultural adaptation on the mission field, or ministry. These kinds of problems can negatively impact the missionary, the mission agency, and the "cause of world missions."[17] Later in the book, Rodolfo Giron writes on how the "best missionary" is one who understands the Bible well, grasps the role of the church, and who relates well with indigenous people and treats them with respect.[18] Kath Donovan and Ruth Myors note the critical

15. Taylor, "Introduction," 10.
16. Limpic, "Brazilian Missionaries," 148.
17. McKaughan, "Missionary Attrition," 18.
18. Giron, "Integrated Model of Missions," 34.

nature of rigorously learning the host language for a period in the foreign land upon arrival.[19]

Examining literature that deals with missionary attrition for "New Sending Countries" (NSC), the most frequent reason for NSC attrition, just over 8 percent of NSC attrition cases, is deficiency of home financial and other support. The number two reason for NSC attrition is "lack of call" (8 percent of NSC attrition cases).[20] Once on the field, missionaries realize they misinterpreted a call to missions, or they lose any call they had when they left their home country. Other common causes of attrition for NSC missionaries are: "inadequate commitment," in that the missionary was unable to persevere longer term in the mission work and life (7.3 percent); disagreement with their mission agency (6.1 percent); problems with missionary teammates (5.7 percent); underdeveloped spiritual life (4.5 percent); insufficient training (4.5 percent); and, difficulties adapting cross-culturally (3 percent).

In addition to William Taylor's edited book on the findings of WEA's ReMAP in 1997 are the findings of WEA's ReMAP II, *Worth Keeping*, which was edited by Rob Hay and published in 2007. In writing an article based on the findings of ReMAP II, Detlef Blocher writes how critical for a high retaining mission agency is "a culture of prayer" and utilizing "careful candidate selection."[21] Analyzing leadership within the agency, high retaining agencies emphasize having: methods for missionaries to voice complaints; solid on-field supervision; and, leaders identifying problems early and resolving them.[22] Again highlighted is the need of having intensive language study.[23] High retaining agencies allow missionaries to properly balance work and rest, and one's personal relationship with the Lord.[24]

ReMAP and ReMAP II provide data from their research that reveal the most important factors that correlate with lower avoidable attrition. The data from ReMAP I shows how mission agencies that required the following pre-field preparation had a markedly lower attrition rate: cross-cultural orientation; theological education; cross-cultural experience; degree in

---

19. Donovan and Myors, "Reflections on Attrition," 58.
20. Brierley, "Missionary Attrition," 94.
21. Blocher, "Good Agency Practices," 231.
22. Blocher, "Good Agency Practices," 231–32.
23. Blocher, "Good Agency Practices," 232.
24. Blocher, "Good Agency Practices," 233.

missiology; and, mission studies, informal or formal.[25] There is correlation between if they received these trainings and if attrition was reduced. In ReMAP II, higher retaining agencies followed these practices to minimize preventable attrition: greater importance on screening; pre-field training; good communication practices; greater emphasis on prayer; ongoing training opportunities; care practices; and, leadership practices.[26] Again, those agencies that emphasized these components had higher retention of their missionaries. The findings from ReMAP and ReMAP II raise the question as to reasons for avoidable attrition of Chinese missionaries. These studies inform my approach to investigating the experience of Chinese missionaries who have remained on the field. We will return to the ReMAP and ReMAP II studies in the literature review, and how they show a correlation between pre-field training and missionary retention.

Majority World Mission Challenges

The Chinese mission movement is a majority world mission movement. "Majority world" denotes primarily countries in Asia, Africa, and South America. In previous eras, majority world was also referred to as "third world," "two-thirds world," and "global south." Since the Chinese mission movement is a majority world mission movement, of relevance for analyzing and understanding Chinese missionaries is to have an understanding of common themes and challenges for majority world missions, more generally.

Generally speaking, majority world mission movements have remained smaller without forming well-structured mission agencies or associations. Roger E. Hedlund underscores the significance of majority world mission movements forming mission structures.[27] Timothy Park listed as a strength of the Korean movement that they founded mission committees and organizations.[28] COMIBAM is the chief mission umbrella organization in Latin America. COMIBAM is an acronym for "Cooperacion Misionera Ibero-Americana" ["Ibero-American Missionary Cooperation"].[29] It was through COMIBAM, not itself a mission agency but a mission network

---

25. Blocher and Lewis, "Further Findings," 113.
26. World Evangelical Alliance Missions Commission, "ReMAP II," 17.
27. Hedlund, "Structures and Patterns," 29–32.
28. Park, "Korean Christian World Mission," 166.
29. Guarneri, "COMIBAM," 221.

of mission agencies, that Latin American missions accelerated in effectiveness and missionaries sent. The closest Africa has to Latin America's continent-wide effective mission association COMIBAM is the Association of Evangelicals in Africa (AEA). However, AEA desires to reach all of Africa rather than the entire world. A continent-wide African mission association facilitating missions both inside and outside Africa could benefit the African mission efforts, as COMIBAM has significantly aided the Latin American mission movement.

Howard Brant lists "sustainable finances" as the prime hindrance to majority world missions.[30] The Korean mission movement was aided by economic growth, and hence was able to increase missionary sending (Moon 2016, 6-7; Park 2010, 167-169).[31] Korean[32] (Cho 1979, 92), Brazilian[33] (Limpic 1997, 149), African[34] (Turaki 2000, 281), and Indian[35] (Rajendran 2010, 73) mission movements have all at some point in time been hindered by a dearth of finances. Korea is the only region studied that at present is a "wealthy" place. The other three, Latin America, Africa, and India, all are "poorer" regions, and must address the challenge of sufficient capital for world missions. The Ghana Evangelical Missions Association has used micro financing to raise money for missions (Anyomi 2010, 49).[36] The early years of Friends Missionary Prayer Band had Indian Christian prayer group members each donating small amounts of money.[37] If a country is impoverished, the Christians there may lack funds to send missionaries to other countries. Nevertheless, some poor countries (e.g. India) spend less money on missionary sending by sending missionaries cross-culturally within India, or to geographically closer countries. Or missionaries from poorer contexts can be "tentmakers" and work on the mission field, so they do not need to rely on receiving money from their home country. The traditional mission method for Western missionaries has been raising funds. Doing this is harder for majority world missionaries from poorer countries.

---

30. Brant, "Seven Essentials," 50.

31. Moon, *Korean Missionary Movement*, 6-7; Park, "Missionary Movement of the Korean Church," 167-69.

32. Cho, "Diagnostic Survey of Missionary Movement in Korea," 92.

33. Limpic, "Brazilian Missionaries," 149.

34. Turaki, "Evangelical Missiology from Africa," 281.

35. Rajendran, "Emergence and Expansion of Indian Mission," 73.

36. Anyomi, "African Missionary Movement," 49.

37. Hedlund, "Friends Missionary Prayer Band," 100.

Similarly, effective training is essential for majority world mission movements. In commenting on the WEA's research on missionary attrition, Blocher wrote, "High retaining [mission] agencies expect twice as much theological education from their missionary candidates and three times as much formal missiological training than low retaining [mission] agencies."[38] Training is a monumental influence in missionary attrition. Indian Evangelical Mission candidates in training studied courses such as "linguistics, anthropology, evangelism, religions, village health care, and bookkeeping."[39] Training of Latin American missionaries consists of 200 mission training centers, and the publishing of a best practices guide for missionary training in Latin America.[40] Blocher's writing shows that the research reveals that generally speaking effectual missionary training leads to retention and effectiveness on the mission field. Majority world missionaries have to be well trained pre-field and after being on the field.

Large mission congresses and conferences can aid the majority world mission movement in that context. One of COMIBAM's contributions to the Latin American mission movement has been its forming of numerous mission congresses.[41] The establishment of Indian mission structures began with the Evangelical Fellowship of India (EFI) evangelical congresses beginning in the 1950s and later EFI-organized mission congresses.[42] These conferences assist spreading the message of the urgency of world missions. They facilitate people interested in missions meeting each other for the purpose of cooperation. Such conferences spread mission fervor to indigenous pastors and churches. Korean[43] and Latin American[44] mission experts explain the impact of global international congresses such as the Lausanne Congress in 1974 on the founding of comparable congresses in their context, and how the subsequent congresses in their own context spurred their mission efforts.

Many majority world missionaries end up ministering to persons from their homeland that live abroad. There is certainly a need for that. But if the vision of the sending churches is to reach the unreached of other

38. Blocher, "Good Agency Practices," 231.
39. Hedlund, "Indian Evangelical Mission," 480.
40. Carvalho, "Latin American Missionary Movement," 66.
41. Deiros, "COMIBAM," 211–12.
42. Rajendran, "Emergence and Expansion of Indian Mission," 63.
43. Park, "Missionary Movement of the Korean Church," 167–69.
44. Guarneri, "COMIBAM," 227–31.

ethnicities, then such work does not fulfill that vision. Korean mission leaders no longer count ministering among Korean diaspora and ministering cross-culturally in Korea as "missionaries."[45] Anecdotal reports (and through my conversations with some Chinese contacted for this research who are known in China as "missionaries," but who are not ministering cross-culturally in the foreign country) indicate that numerous Chinese "missionaries" go abroad to reach the hosts; but after arrival, they realize the difficulties in cross-cultural ministry, and eventually minister to Chinese in the foreign land. If cross-cultural ministry is the original intent of the missionary and home mission agency, the missionary's mission agency has to hold that missionary accountable to minister cross-culturally on the mission field. The missionaries must persevere through initial challenges in connecting with the indigenous people, that fruitful ministry and relationships with them may ensue.

Korean[46] and African[47] experts articulated how their country's government's diplomatic relationships abroad facilitated missionary sending. The Chinese government, now doing wide-ranging trade in Central Asia, the Middle East, and North Africa, has amiable relationships with various predominantly Muslim countries. These strong diplomatic relationships that the Chinese government has with Muslim country governments open doors for Chinese missionaries to move to those countries to work and do ministry to Muslims.

How paramount is a high level of education for majority world missionaries? Park claims that the Korean mission movement was partly successful because of emphasizing education.[48] If missionary candidates cannot speak English or another foreign language, they may have difficulties learning a new language on the mission field. It can be beneficial for majority world missionaries to have a bachelor's degree. A challenge for missionaries now from around the world is that "closed" countries do not grant a missionary visa. These missionaries must seek employment in that context, to obtain a visa. A missionary without a bachelor's degree may be strained to find a job on the mission field. The experts on majority world missions fail to mention how the missionaries from their region obtain visas in "closed" countries, if they get jobs, have student visas, or start a business.

45. Park, "Korean Christian World Mission," 100–102.
46. Park, "Missionary Movement of the Korean Church," 169.
47. Adeyemo, "Profiling," 267.
48. Park, "Missionary Movement of the Korean Church," 169.

Research Problem and Research Questions

Research Problem: There is a widespread impression that attrition among Chinese missionaries is exceptionally high. This is commonly attributed to poor adjustment to the host culture. Therefore this dissertation will investigate the research concern of factors impacting cultural adjustment and retention of Chinese cross-cultural workers.

Research Question #1: How are Chinese cross-cultural workers succeeding or struggling with building cross-cultural relationships?

Sub-RQ #1.1: Is there evidence for the dominant impression about Chinese cross-cultural workers' difficulty in cross-cultural communication?

Sub-RQ #1.2: How have Chinese cross-cultural workers attempted to adapt in learning the host language and assimilating to the host context and culture?

Sub-RQ #1.3: Are there any perceived factors that contribute to those more thriving cross-cultural workers developing effective cross-cultural relationships on the field?

Research Question #2: How have the pre-field and on the field experiences of Chinese cross-cultural workers contributed to retention?

Sub-RQ #2.1: What pre-field preparation or on the field support has been useful for Chinese cross-cultural workers?

Sub-RQ #2.2: What pre-field preparation or on the field support do Chinese cross-cultural workers wish they had received but have not?

Sub-RQ #2.3: What kinds of other support structures (e.g. teammates' support, mission agency leadership, mission field leadership, conferences, other trainings) have helped contribute to cross-cultural workers' retention?

Sub-RQ #2.4: What other specific factors have contributed to retention?

INTRODUCTION

Significance of the Research and Anticipated New Contribution

From a missiological standpoint, as a result of this research, those interested in Chinese missions can have a deeper grasp of the Chinese mission movement. Some within the Chinese mission movement can use the conclusions and research from this dissertation to modify how Chinese mission agencies are run, so that these agencies may be more effective and fruitful. Some promoters of the Chinese mission movement have exaggerated and overly optimistic expectations, and have failed to take into account challenges that Chinese missionaries have been facing. This research provides a portrayal of what is happening in Chinese missions. It could be encouraging and pertinent to those Chinese or foreign Christians within China directly involved in or supportive of Chinese missions.

An additional missiological point of significance in this research is that the Chinese mission movement is in a unique situation. China is a country that is not just a majority world country with an emerging movement, but Chinese missionaries are coming from a place where the majority of sending churches are not registered and thus illegal, facing government restrictions or outright opposition. Their sending structures are not able to publicly and legally have a mission agency office or mission training facilities in China, or hold mission conferences within China. A challenge for Chinese missionaries unique from most other majority world missionaries is that the Chinese government will not approve their visa to live in another country, if the Chinese government suspects they are doing mission work or ministry in that foreign country. The Chinese government will not approve Chinese people having "missionary visas" in other countries. In addition, the last two years the Chinese government has increased surveillance and persecution of house churches in China, which means the government has also increased surveillance of suspected Chinese missionaries or interrogating them when they return to China. These dynamics add challenges for Chinese missionaries.

The last ten or twenty years, people have written about Chinese missions,[49] but few if any have explained or studied in detail Chinese missionaries' experiences. Research conducted for this dissertation was unable to discover any published empirical research. The only academic

---

49. See Ro, "Rising Missions Movement in China"; Lee, "Mission China"; Yao, "Chinese Church."

research located about Chinese missions is a Doctor of Ministry (DMin) dissertation by Wang Kay Chan in 2012.[50] It is not written in English, but rather traditional Chinese characters. Chan's paper is about Chinese missionary training and oversight; it lacks empirical research. It focuses on "Chinese" Christians worldwide, rather than those sent from Mainland China. A Master of Divinity (MDiv) thesis about Chinese missions was written in 1985 by Henry T. Ang.[51] But this paper as an MDiv thesis deals only with theoretical themes in Chinese missions, and is not based upon empirical research. The emphasis is on Chinese churches around the world sending missionaries.

Another contribution of this dissertation is to help inform the pre-field preparation of Chinese missionary candidates. From the findings from this dissertation, those involved in missions from China may be better informed about the needs and challenges of Chinese missionaries, and how pre-field training or other factors contribute to retention and effectiveness in cross-cultural adjustment for Chinese missionaries.

Theoretical Construct and Definition of Terms

This dissertation addresses theories related to missionary attrition, in particular avoidable reasons why missionaries prematurely leave the field. Using interviews this research explores reasons for Chinese missionary retention, with a focus upon the factor of relationship building in the host culture.

The theories and data that inform this research consist of four domains of literature: sources related directly to missionary training, sources related to missionary attrition, sources related to cross-cultural relationships and adjustment, and sources related to the church in China. These will be described in the following chapter.

As demonstrated in the literature review in chapter 2, there is a general consensus that effectively building cross-cultural relationships includes: reducing and managing anxiety and uncertainty; being a "good listener"; avoiding having an ethnocentric mindset; a willingness to "self-disclose" to others; knowing the indigenous culture well; learning to speak the host language well; and, often adopting indigenous behaviors and customs.

50. Chan, "On the Nurturing."
51. Ang, "Role of the Chinese Church."

Cross-cultural workers who evidence healthy adjustment in these ways will be considered "flourishing" in this dissertation.

Literature about missionary attrition is mostly from the WEA's two landmark studies on missionary attrition, ReMAP and ReMAP II. This data is compared to the experiences of Chinese missionaries interviewed, with a concentration on what factors have contributed to Chinese missionaries' retention on the mission field. As both the ReMAP and ReMAP II research findings are dated, these are not to be relied on too heavily. However, this research constitutes what we do know about missionary attrition. Its research and conclusions are still relevant and helpful. Precedent literature on missionary training focuses on missionary training's relationship to missionary retention. Also covered is how missionary training pertains to cross-cultural adjustment.

As stated above, "Chinese missionary" in this dissertation refers to Chinese missionaries from Mainland China, which excludes those from Hong Kong, Macau, Taiwan or Chinese churches worldwide (Chinese diaspora). They are serving outside of China. They are not ministering to Chinese living in that place, but are ministering among host non-Chinese people living in that context.

"Effective cross-cultural relationships" in this dissertation are interpersonal relationships characterized by mutual trust, self-disclosure, low levels of anxiety and uncertainty, "good" listening, a nonjudgmental attitude towards one another, and knowledge of each other's culture.

"Host culture" refers to the culture in which the missionary is living and ministering, which is outside the missionary's own home context.

"Hosts" are those people in the foreign land who belong to the host culture.

Though "cross-cultural" and "intercultural" technically have different meanings, they are used interchangeably in this dissertation.

"On the field," "on-field," or "on the mission field" refer to missionaries being in their mission context living outside their home country.

"Pre-field" is something that occurs before the missionary has moved to the mission field.

Limitations and Delimitations

A limitation of this research is that it was impossible to do onsite interviews, as the interviewees are in different countries. Another limitation is that, due to security concerns, there may have been reluctance for Chinese missionaries to participate in the research. An additional limitation is that I was limited to people who were willing to give me names and contact information of Chinese missionaries. Another limitation is that the interviewees' responses were simply based on their subjective perceptions. A delimitation is that this research only examined a small qualitative research sample of Chinese missionaries. A delimitation was to only concentrate on long-term Chinese missionaries, rather than short-term. Only Mainland Chinese missionaries who minister cross-culturally to reach hosts in that context were researched, and not those ministering among Chinese in the foreign land. Missionaries from Taiwan, Hong Kong, Macau, or Chinese churches outside China were not studied; rather the target was on Chinese missionaries connected to house churches in Mainland China. Another delimitation is that only Chinese missionaries who have been commissioned by a sending church as missionaries were researched, who are serving in a mission agency or were sent as missionaries through a house church network. This did not include Chinese Christian businessmen who live and work abroad but are not commissioned as missionaries from China.

Structure

The monograph has six chapters. The first chapter is related to the research problem and explains the importance of the research question, which includes a definition of key terms. The second chapter is a review of relevant literature. The third chapter describes the methodology of the study. This consists of a detailed explanation and description of the methodological approach, as well as any challenges or ethical issues in the study. Chapter four reports the findings from the interviews from the research. The fifth chapter is analysis of the research findings. Also included are major implications from the study. The sixth chapter is recommendations and final conclusions from the research.

2

Precedent Literature

IN THIS SECTION, THE precedent literature on building effective cross-cultural relationships will be reviewed first, followed by literature on missionary attrition. Missionary training literature will then be evaluated, followed by literature on the church in China. Finally, how this dissertation addresses themes in the existing literature of these four topics will be presented.

Effectively Building Relationships Cross-Culturally

This section discusses the effective building of cross-cultural relationships. To fully understand this topic, it is necessary to examine this subject from both secular and Christian perspectives. This dissertation will examine primarily secular scholars who write from a research-based standpoint. Of particular interest for this dissertation is the topic of how to effectively build relationships cross-culturally. Chinese missionaries were interviewed regarding their experiences on the mission field in building such relationships. In this part, secular sources will be discussed first, followed by Christian sources and then a comparison of the two approaches.

Secular Sources

The most influential secular sources consulted for this section are William B. Gudykunst, Myron W. Lustig and Jolene Koester, and Carley H. Dodd. These writers have an academic audience in mind; all of their books are research-based and technical in nature. Gudykunst, a scholar of intercultural communication, is renowned in his field for developing the "Anxiety/Uncertainty Management" (AUM) theory. Lustig and Koester are authorities on intercultural competence. One of Dodd's noteworthy contributions has been on how the "Homophily Principle" affects intercultural communication.

William B. Gudykunst

In their book *Communicating with Strangers*, William B. Gudykunst and Young Yun Kim discuss how to effectively communicate with strangers. They note that the key to effective communication is to reduce confusion.[1] Cultural differences have their source in people's "motivation, knowledge, and skills."[2] They describe one's "motivation" as including a "need for predictability," which is the desire to have interaction with others that is predictable and without surprises[3]; unpredictable exchanges lead one to feel "diffuse anxiety," which stems from "deprivations in meeting our needs for security, predictability, group inclusion, and self-confirmation."[4] We are to be mindful of others' self-conceptions and what is significant in their idea of self as well as how we can avoid retreating from strangers and just interacting with those who are like us.[5]

The second variation between cultures that impacts communication is "knowledge." This is described as how we take in information about others,[6] including both knowledge of the differences between our own group and an outside group and knowledge of ways we may be like others.[7] We are to be "mindful of our communication" and think about outsiders' perspectives, not just our own.[8] The third component that influences our communication is our "skills," including how we "manage uncertainty and anxiety."[9] Gudykunst and Kim summarize the following skills which are important to effective intercultural communication: being mindful of how we communicate and how others' communicate[10]; having a high "tolerance

---

1. Gudykunst and Kim, *Communicating with Strangers*, 269.
2. Gudykunst and Kim, *Communicating with Strangers*, 276.
3. Gudykunst and Kim, *Communicating with Strangers*, 276–77.
4. Gudykunst and Kim, *Communicating with Strangers*, 277.
5. Gudykunst and Kim, *Communicating with Strangers*, 278.
6. Gudykunst and Kim, *Communicating with Strangers*, 280.
7. Gudykunst and Kim, *Communicating with Strangers*, 281–82.
8. Gudykunst and Kim, *Communicating with Strangers*, 283.
9. Gudykunst and Kim, *Communicating with Strangers*, 285.
10. Gudykunst and Kim, *Communicating with Strangers*, 287.

for ambiguity"[11]; being able to overcome anxious thoughts[12] and empathize with others; and not following the "Golden Rule" (Do unto others as you would have them do unto you), but the "Platinum Rule" (Do unto others as they would have you do unto them).[13] Making correct predictions and explanations of strangers' behavior is also critical.[14]

Expectations, which influence interactions with strangers, can sometimes lead us to avoid strangers, at least until we experience positive interaction with them.[15] Again noting the AUM, communicating with those like us leads to less uncertainty than when communicating with those unlike us. Communication with those of other ethnic groups often increases our anxiety.[16] With decreased anxiety and uncertainty, however, we have greater "perceived quality and effectiveness of communication."[17] Thus, comprehending the host culture and language aids us in developing interpersonal relationships. One key in comprehending interpersonal relationships is "*perceived* similarity between others," rather than simply actual likeness in cultural, racial, or other ways. In comparison to "intracultural" interactions (with people of the same culture), intercultural interactions generally lead to less self-disclosure to the other, perceptiveness of the other, and receptiveness of the other.[18] In order to develop initial interactions into friendships, we need to communicate with others, have a knowledge of their culture, sense a "degree of similarity" between us and them, and show them we are not "negative stereotyping" them.[19]

Gudykunst further articulates his AUM theory in some of his other works. In his 1988 book *Theories in Intercultural Communication*, he illuminates his theories behind uncertainty and anxiety. Charles R. Berger in 1979 wrote how the Uncertainty Reduction Theory proposes that people in certain situations try to reduce uncertainty in interactions with strangers.[20] Elsewhere, Gudykunst explains, "Effective communication is moderated

11. Gudykunst and Kim, *Communicating with Strangers*, 288.
12. Gudykunst and Kim, *Communicating with Strangers*, 289.
13. Gudykunst and Kim, *Communicating with Strangers*, 290.
14. Gudykunst and Kim, *Communicating with Strangers*, 292–93.
15. Gudykunst and Kim, *Communicating with Strangers*, 338.
16. Gudykunst and Kim, *Communicating with Strangers*, 339.
17. Gudykunst and Kim, *Communicating with Strangers*, 341.
18. Gudykunst and Kim, *Communicating with Strangers*, 344–45.
19. Gudykunst and Kim, *Communicating with Strangers*, 346.
20. Gudykunst, "Uncertainty and Anxiety," 123–24.

by our ability to mindfully manage our anxiety and reduce our uncertainty about ourselves and the people with whom we are communicating."[21] In a later work, Gudykunst himself explains that he first used the term "Anxiety/Uncertainty Management (AUM) Theory" in 1993.[22]

In his book *Bridging Differences*, Gudykunst indicates how the perception process sways the way we attribute meaning to strangers. Often we assume that our perception and observation of strangers is unbiased.[23] Likewise, when we delineate categories to those around us, we further alienate them from us.[24] If we hold to narrow categories of others, we cannot make sense of the limitations and inaccuracies of our categories.[25] Instead, we should strive to correctly interpret others' behaviors by evaluating why they act in certain ways rather than just relying on our experiences.[26] If correct, our social attributions of outsiders can help us interpret their behavior.[27] However, our prejudices towards outsiders can obscure our perceptions when strangers behave in a way we deem immoral.[28]

Gudykunst clarifies how our unique cultural perspectives lead to misinterpretations of outsiders' behavior.[29] Two ways that cultural perceptions lead to confusion in cross-cultural interaction are factors related to differences in individualistic and collectivistic cultures and differences between high-context and low-context communication.[30] Personality also influences how we interpret others' behavior, including the category width of our perceptions of them,[31] the extent to which we have an open or closed mind,[32] and the complexity of our thinking.[33]

Gudykunst and Sudweeks in 1992 articulate intercultural adaptation. They stress the importance of understanding the outsiders' culture

21. Gudykunst, "Toward a Theory," 37–38.
22. Gudykunst, "Anxiety/Uncertainty Management," 9.
23. Gudykunst, *Bridging Differences*, 160.
24. Gudykunst, *Bridging Differences*, 161.
25. Gudykunst, *Bridging Differences*, 163.
26. Gudykunst, *Bridging Differences*, 166.
27. Gudykunst, *Bridging Differences*, 167.
28. Gudykunst, *Bridging Differences*, 168.
29. Gudykunst, *Bridging Differences*, 169.
30. Gudykunst, *Bridging Differences*, 171.
31. Gudykunst, *Bridging Differences*, 174.
32. Gudykunst, *Bridging Differences*, 175.
33. Gudykunst, *Bridging Differences*, 178.

and language and having accurate "stereotypes" of their culture.[34] They suggest that we describe others' behavior, rather than trying to evaluate their behavior.[35] They describe detrimental ways of coping with anxiety and stress in a new culture as including criticism of the other culture and avoiding interacting with people from that culture.[36] Instead, they recommend being flexible in intercultural encounters and adapting our behavior appropriately to the native context. In their article "Strangers and Hosts: An Uncertainty Reduction Based Theory of Intercultural Adaptation," Gudykunst and Hammer also address intercultural adaptation. Some of their germane axioms are that knowing the host culture decreases our uncertainty and that an increase in prejudice and ethnocentrism encumbers "predicting" the host peoples' behavior.[37]

Myron W. Lustig and Jolene Koester

Myron W. Lustig and Jolene Koester, in their influential book *Intercultural Competence: Interpersonal Communication across Cultures*, elucidate how to effectively build relationships cross-culturally. In their chapter about intercultural competence, the authors specify three terms defining interpersonal relationships: "strangers," "acquaintances," and "friends."[38] For this dissertation, the most relevant terminology is that of "friend," a person with whom we have a closer bond that has a "higher level of intimacy, self-disclosure, involvement, intensity," commitment and trust.[39]

Learning about people from other cultures has manifold components. A high level of unpredictability exists in intercultural relationships as multiple stimuli can cause anxiety: fears about one's future interaction with someone; distress about having an inferior interaction with those perceived as outsiders; and, someone perceiving another person as having a low degree of predictability.[40] Negative consequences occur when people neglect to be "mindful" of others.[41]

34. Gudykunst and Sudweeks, "Applying a Theory," 358.
35. Gudykunst and Sudweeks, "Applying a Theory," 359.
36. Gudykunst and Sudweeks, "Applying a Theory," 365.
37. Gudykunst and Hammer, "Strangers and Hosts," 115–16.
38. Lustig and Koester, *Among US*, 225.
39. Lustig and Koester, *Among US*, 227–28.
40. Lustig and Koester, *Intercultural Competence*, 241–42.
41. Lustig and Koester, *Intercultural Competence*, 242–44.

Self-disclosure varies from culture to culture, including what content is shared and when it is shared. Part of this self-disclosure is the "breadth" of what kind of information is shared between people, that is, the subjects that people share. The "depth" of the self-disclosure signifies how personal the information is that is shared. The "timing" of the self-disclosure is the stage in the relationship self-disclosure will occur. In addition to these, there is also the "target" of the self-disclosure, who is the recipient of the self-disclosure.[42]

In another book *AmongUS*, Lustig and Koester explain ethnocentrism. We learn about right and wrong through our upbringing. This naturally leads us to think that anyone unlike us is wrong.[43] When we have ethnocentric thoughts towards outsiders, we react in an impassioned manner to dissimilar characteristics between them and us and we thus are incapable of having positive interactions with them.[44] The "competent intercultural communicator" is able to handle ethnocentric thoughts and reactions and be unimpeded by them.[45] "Prejudice" is "negative attitudes toward other people that are based on faulty and inflexible stereotypes."[46] A suggested technique in endeavoring to improve our intercultural communication is to think about ways we place others into categories. We can reflect on positive and negative stereotypes and categories about others and form a list of those stereotypes, helping us to be aware of them.[47]

Carley H. Dodd

Carley H. Dodd, in *Dynamics of Intercultural Communication*, notes products of having high intercultural competencies and effectiveness, which include adapting to a new place and building strong relationships with host residents.[48] Tips for intercultural effectiveness are: focus on whatever resemblances exist between you and that person, have an open mind about those who are different, and be a good listener and show concern for others.[49] In

---

42. Lustig and Koester, *Intercultural Competence*, 244–45.
43. Lustig and Koester, *Among US*, 158.
44. Lustig and Koester, *Among US*, 159.
45. Lustig and Koester, *Among US*, 160.
46. Lustig and Koester, *Among US*, 164.
47. Lustig and Koester, *Among US*, 169.
48. Dodd, *Dynamics of Intercultural Communication*, 173.
49. Dodd, *Dynamics of Intercultural Communication*, 183.

another chapter, which addresses intercultural communication and conflict, Dodd mentions how self-disclosure is usually nonexistent between casual friends, but instead occurs within close relationships. Americans generally only self-disclose information if they trust the listeners. Each culture has varying ideas about what should be shared in relationships and when self-disclosure should happen.[50] In intercultural situations, a conflict stemming from self-disclosure can happen when an imbalanced amount of self-disclosure is shared between parties and someone is offended.[51]

Ways to improve intercultural communication include nonjudgmentally accepting others and having a sense of empathy for others' desires.[52] Being a good listener and having "relational empathy" facilitate managing conflict cross-culturally.[53] Reasons are numerous why people may be bad listeners. People may not pay close attention to what is being said. When someone's words seem strange to us, we may try to ignore or confuse the part of the message that we oppose.[54]

Later in the book, Dodd describes the "Homophily Principle," which is "the tendency to communicate with those similar to us."[55] This refers to people who possess comparable physical characteristics, backgrounds, attitudes, values, and personality.[56] When sharing information with those like us, effective communication ensues; people are likely to accept a message if they perceive likenesses between the speaker and themselves.[57] We tend to be in groups with those like us.[58] Though that is the case, Dodd also clarifies, "We learn, grow, and develop when interaction includes some differences."[59]

Dodd explains intercultural effectiveness. One outcome of effectiveness is building deeper relationships with others (1987, 3).[60] Several variables can be used for predicting intercultural effectiveness. For example, boastful

---

50. Dodd, *Dynamics of Intercultural Communication*, 189.
51. Dodd, *Dynamics of Intercultural Communication*, 189–90.
52. Dodd, *Dynamics of Intercultural Communication*, 193.
53. Dodd, *Dynamics of Intercultural Communication*, 202.
54. Dodd, *Dynamics of Intercultural Communication*, 203.
55. Dodd, *Dynamics of Intercultural Communication*, 209.
56. Dodd, *Dynamics of Intercultural Communication*, 209–11.
57. Dodd, *Dynamics of Intercultural Communication*, 211.
58. Dodd, *Dynamics of Intercultural Communication*, 214–15.
59. Dodd, *Dynamics of Intercultural Communication*, 215.
60. Dodd, "Introduction," 3.

people generally struggle with poor intercultural communication. Ethnocentrism is a large hindrance to intercultural communication, as is an inflexible attitude.[61] Having a heart of empathy and an attitude of openness towards others, however, usually leads to superior intercultural interaction.[62]

Christian Sources

Christian writers on the subject of intercultural competency include Duane Elmer, Sherwood Lingenfelter, and Scott Moreau and others. Duane Elmer's books *Cross-Cultural Connections* and *Cross-Cultural Servanthood* are on building relationships cross-culturally. Sherwood Lingenfelter and Marvin Mayers wrote the prominent book *Ministering Cross-Culturally* in 1986, which is now in its third printing and has been widely used by missionary trainers and in academic settings over the past thirty-three years. Scott Moreau has written many influential books on various topics about missions. For this dissertation, I consulted his recent multi-authored nearly 400-page book *Effective Intercultural Communication*.[63]

Duane Elmer

In Duane Elmer's 2006 book *Cross-Cultural Servanthood*, he notes dynamics relevant to building relationships across cultures as well as how to be a cross-cultural servant. In his books, he writes anecdotally to a popular audience and does not base his writings on his own empirical research. The idea of "servanthood" varies from culture to culture; upon arrival in a new context, "servanthood" may be displayed in learning about the host culture and beginning to learn the language.[64]

Elmer explicates the importance of "openness," which he defines as "the ability to welcome people into your presence and make them feel safe."[65] This "openness" is directed towards people similar to us or different from us. We are to treat other humans with respect because they are made

---

61. Dodd, "Introduction," 6.
62. Dodd, "Introduction," 7.
63. Moreau, *Effective Intercultural Communication*.
64. Elmer, *Cross-Cultural Servanthood*, 13.
65. Elmer, *Cross-Cultural Servanthood*, 39.

in God's image.[66] The author suggests several ways to promote openness. When we "suspend judgment," it prevents us from forming incorrect conclusions.[67] If we have a "tolerance of ambiguity," we can persevere in the midst of confusing situations and slowly comprehend the host culture.[68] We can "think gray" by not immediately forming an opinion about a situation but instead "suspending judgment" and eventually obtaining an accurate interpretation. When we seek to assume the best scenario in an unknown situation, we strive for "positive attribution."

"Acceptance" is "the ability to communicate value, worth and esteem to another person."[69] We can accept people from other cultures based on God's creation of them in his own image.[70] Five main factors may limit our ability to accept others. The first is disregarding learning their language.[71] The second and third are to have an impatient attitude and an ethnocentric mindset towards others.[72] The fourth, "category width," pertains to how having narrow cognitive categories can cause us to critically respond to our environment.[73] The fifth is "dogmatism," and how firm and unmoving we may be in our own values and ideals.[74]

Elmer describes "trust," which he defines as "the ability to build confidence in a relationship so that both parties believe the other will not inadvertently hurt them but will act in their best interest."[75] Building trust takes ample time.[76] It is risky when we attempt to reach out to others, as we do not know if the relationship will turn out well or not. Vital is trust "being nurtured"; this necessitates a constant commitment to retain and build trust in a relationship.[77] A suggestion on building trust cross-culturally is to intentionally be aware that how we establish trust in our

---

66. Elmer, *Cross-Cultural Servanthood*, 45.
67. Elmer, *Cross-Cultural Servanthood*, 51.
68. Elmer, *Cross-Cultural Servanthood*, 54.
69. Elmer, *Cross-Cultural Servanthood*, 58.
70. Elmer, *Cross-Cultural Servanthood*, 63.
71. Elmer, *Cross-Cultural Servanthood*, 66.
72. Elmer, *Cross-Cultural Servanthood*, 67–68.
73. Elmer, *Cross-Cultural Servanthood*, 69.
74. Elmer, *Cross-Cultural Servanthood*, 70.
75. Elmer, *Cross-Cultural Servanthood*, 77.
76. Elmer, *Cross-Cultural Servanthood*, 77–78.
77. Elmer, *Cross-Cultural Servanthood*, 79.

own culture may be contrary to how it is done in the other culture.[78] Trust is tenuous, and it can be detrimental when we lose the trust of those to whom we are ministering.[79]

Elmer emphasizes the importance of "learning," which is defined by Elmer as "the ability to glean relevant information about, from and with other people."[80] First, we are to learn *about* others. Results of learning about others are that we can have a correct picture of a place when we are still new arrivals. This "learning *about* others" step can be done while still comfortably in one's home culture, and may include interacting with others who have lived in the new culture before, or those who are from that culture.[81] "Learning *from* others" is more influential on the hosts than is learning *about* others. We ask them questions to make sense of their perspective, and what is vital to them. We show a humble and learning spirit in our interactions with them. Learning *from* others can be used to tighten our relationship with the indigenous people and aid us in minimizing our and their "stereotypes, prejudice and racism" towards one other.[82] Skills relevant for intercultural ministry are important. The first is to be a good listener. Not only does this show our love to others, but also, denizens are willing to share about themselves when they perceive we are good listeners.[83]

"Understanding" is "the ability to see patterns of behavior and values that reveal the integrity of a people."[84] It is necessary to examine rationally what causes people to do what they do; otherwise, we will struggle to build strong relationships with those around us.[85] When we grasp other cultures well, we can blend in with the residents and get a new perspective on the world.[86] Hindrances for our mastery of the host culture and people are: "egocentrism," the belief that what we do is superior; and, "ethnocentrism."[87] "Perspectivism" is getting to know native people well. Through "perspectivism," we can eliminate our prejudices, build tight

---

78. Elmer, *Cross-Cultural Servanthood*, 81.
79. Elmer, *Cross-Cultural Servanthood*, 83.
80. Elmer, *Cross-Cultural Servanthood*, 93.
81. Elmer, *Cross-Cultural Servanthood*, 95–96.
82. Elmer, *Cross-Cultural Servanthood*, 97–98.
83. Elmer, *Cross-Cultural Servanthood*, 122.
84. Elmer, *Cross-Cultural Servanthood*, 125.
85. Elmer, *Cross-Cultural Servanthood*, 126.
86. Elmer, *Cross-Cultural Servanthood*, 131.
87. Elmer, *Cross-Cultural Servanthood*, 131–32.

bonds with hosts, have host friends to share life with, and acquire an appreciation of that culture and context.[88]

In Elmer's book *Cross-Cultural Connections* he elucidates his recommended usage of the terms "right, wrong, and different." The chapter's purpose is "to reveal and help reverse that subtle superiority that so many of us unconsciously carry."[89] When we enter a new culture we are met with new surroundings: everything around us is foreign to us. Our first response may be to characterize everything unknown as "bad."[90] It is critical to delay quickly determining what is "good" and "bad" in the new context; rather, we should strive to decipher why we initially assess something as "wrong." We are to attempt to judge insights into the new culture as "different," instead of "bad" or "wrong." This prevents us from having quick judgments about the "strange" observations around us.[91] Our own culture impacts how we behave and see the world.[92] When we seek to comprehend others, sometimes by means of asking them questions about what they do, it prevents us from having a quick judgment of them.[93]

In Elmer's book *Cross-Cultural Conflict*, he clarifies how hosts had a surface level knowledge of missionaries because the missionaries covered up their struggles and weaknesses.[94] This example shows the importance of "self-disclosure" in cross-cultural relationships, which Gudykunst and Kim, Lustig and Koestig, and Dodd underscore.

Sherwood G. Lingenfelter

Concerning Sherwood Lingenfelter and Marvin Mayers' book *Ministering Cross-Culturally*, Lingenfelter is the primary author of this book; Mayers is listed as a co-author because the "model of basic values" originated with him, and he gave feedback on Lingenfelter's book.[95]

---

88. Elmer, *Cross-Cultural Servanthood*, 136.
89. Elmer, *Cross-Cultural Connections*, 22.
90. Elmer, *Cross-Cultural Connections*, 29.
91. Elmer, *Cross-Cultural Connections*, 30–31.
92. Elmer, *Cross-Cultural Connections*, 39.
93. Elmer, *Cross-Cultural Connections*, 40.
94. Elmer, *Cross-Cultural Conflict*, 157.
95. Lingenfelter and Mayers, *Ministering Cross-Culturally*, ix.

The authors describe how Jesus is the metaphor for ministry. Jesus was a "200 percent person," in that he was fully God and fully man.[96] We can become a "150 percent person," which means retaining 75 percent of our own identity and culture while taking on 75 percent of the indigenous culture and identity in which we are ministering. This is to relinquish aspects of our own culture and identity, which shows our love to the residents.[97] This "150 percent person" idea is akin to Paul's words in 1 Corinthians 9:22 to "become all things to all men so that some may be saved."[98]

Lingenfelter and Mayers use Mayers' "model of basic values" from 1974, which contained twelve elements with six pairs of "contrasting priorities for social relationships." The authors clarify how these six contrasting pairs contain opposites on a continuum. Their six values relate to time, judgment, handling crisis, goals, self-worth, and vulnerability. Chapter 3 of this book "Tensions about Time" relates to different perceptions of time in various cultures, and how some cultures are more "punctual" while others are not concerned about time.[99]

In a section titled "Intercultural Competency" in the 2000 *Evangelical Dictionary of World Missions*, Lingenfelter emphasizes the importance of engaging in "cultural learning" in order to become effective cross-culturally in all aspects of life: "effective communication, interpersonal relationships, and continuous learning in a ministry setting."[100] Listed are seven ways that a missionary may become competent in the host culture, which include effective communication using their language, mastering conflict resolution in that context, and having an insight of that culture's values and worldview.[101]

In Lingenfelter's book *Leading Cross-Culturally*, he stresses the importance of learning about the hosts. It is imperative to have expertise in the "social games" of the people, which means to pay careful attention to their ways and habits. This demands the taking of careful notes on what we observe and asking them questions about any confusion.[102] On the topic of learning in a way that builds trust with the denizens, Lingenfelter shares

---

96. Lingenfelter and Mayers, *Ministering Cross-Culturally*, 4–5.
97. Lingenfelter and Mayers, *Ministering Cross-Culturally*, 12.
98. Lingenfelter and Mayers, *Ministering Cross-Culturally*, 14.
99. Lingenfelter and Mayers, *Ministering Cross-Culturally*, 25–38.
100. Lingenfelter, "Intercultural Competency," 494.
101. Lingenfelter, "Intercultural Competency," 494–95.
102. Lingenfelter, *Leading Cross-Culturally*, 64.

through his example of the Aukan leaders about the significance of learning about the other culture.[103]

A. Scott Moreau, Evvy H. Campbell, and Susan Greener

Moreau, Campbell, and Greener's 2014 textbook on intercultural communication, *Effective Intercultural Communication*, has a chapter on "Intercultural Relationships." Moreau, Campbell, and Greener expound upon the necessity in cross-cultural ministry to build close relationships with the hosts.[104] Cross-cultural relationships have three phases. The first is "Initial Uncertainty." This refers to the level of anxiety stemming from initiating a new relationship. A goal at the beginning of a relationship is to decrease the anxiety in initial interactions by "developing shared communication patterns"; this happens through learning the basics about their culture.[105] The second phase of cross-cultural relationships is "Friendly Relations." Ways to accomplish this are letting the people assist you, managing intercultural conflict well, and moving past ways that your cultures are different.[106] The third phase of cross-cultural relationships is "Intimacy/Friendship." Differing cultures have distinctive ideas of what "intimacy" is. Collective cultures desire to spend extensive time together with their friends; those from individualistic cultures prefer to have more time on their own and less time together with friends.[107] An intimate friendship in any culture will eventually require facing forgiveness.[108]

Later in the book is a section about "preserving relationships." Missionaries must strive to maintain and build relationships with people of the host culture, or "genuine ministry is difficult."[109] On preserving relationships, Moreau, Campbell, and Greener have a summation of Duane Elmer's list of dealing with conflict: "Mutually satisfying conflict resolution requires empathy, humility, a strong concern for the others involved, compromise, patience, a willingness to not have to 'be right', flexibility, adaptability, and recognition

---

103. Lingenfelter, *Leading Cross-Culturally*, 64–66.
104. Moreau et al., *Effective Intercultural Communication*, 240.
105. Moreau et al., *Effective Intercultural Communication*, 242.
106. Moreau et al., *Effective Intercultural Communication*, 246–47.
107. Moreau et al., *Effective Intercultural Communication*, 249.
108. Moreau et al., *Effective Intercultural Communication*, 250.
109. Moreau et al., *Effective Intercultural Communication*, 346.

that resolution strategies are culturally bound and that your favored way of addressing conflict may not be appropriate to the context."[110]

Comparison of Approaches

Upon analyzing the main concepts from the sources, many of them mention the influence of "uncertainty" and "anxiety" in intercultural communication. Though Gudykunst had been researching anxiety and uncertainty in intercultural communication for many years, it was not until 1993 that he first penned his theory the "Anxiety/Uncertainty Management (AUM) Theory."[111] Gudykunst and Kim note that when we communicate with those of other ethnic groups, we experience increased anxiety.[112] Having less anxiety and uncertainty results in superior "perceived quality and effectiveness of communication."[113] When we manage anxiety, we can develop trust with indigenous people.[114] Damaging ways we can deal with anxiety and stress cross-culturally are to criticize the host culture and stop interacting with the people.[115] Lustig and Koester mention Gudykunst's AUM: numerous stimuli can cause anxiety for intercultural encounters.[116] Moreau, Campbell, and Greener do not explicitly reference Gudykunst or his AUM; but they seem to be following parallel ideas that reducing anxiety is necessary for the "Initial Uncertainty" that exists in relationships.[117] Moreau, Campbell, and Greener also extensively use the language of "anxiety" and "uncertainty." Reducing uncertainty in a context demands grasping host ideas of "gender roles, social power, status, role, and friendship."[118]

The scholars are also in consensus that being a "good listener" is vital in cross-cultural communication. Gudykunst writes about "listening effectively."[119] We have to be intentional to be effective listeners.[120] We are

110. Moreau et al., *Effective Intercultural Communication*, 347.
111. Gudykunst, "Anxiety/Uncertainty Management," 9.
112. Gudykunst and Kim, *Communicating with Strangers*, 339.
113. Gudykunst and Kim, *Communicating with Strangers*, 341.
114. Gudykunst, *Bridging Differences*, 330.
115. Gudykunst and Sudweeks, "Applying a Theory," 365.
116. Lustig and Koester, *Intercultural Competence*, 241–42.
117. Moreau et al., *Effective Intercultural Communication*, 241–42.
118. Moreau et al., *Effective Intercultural Communication*, 244.
119. Gudykunst, *Bridging Differences*, 182–86.
120. Gudykunst, *Bridging Differences*, 183.

to show the speakers our interest in what they are saying; we let them speak without interrupting, and use "perception checking" by restating to them their words in our own words.[121] Dodd articulates the necessity of practicing "active listening."[122] We cannot "prejudge the message," or "filter out" the parts of the message we disagree with or cannot understand.[123] We must focus intently through the whole message without letting our minds wander.[124] Elmer notes how when we are "good listeners" we not only show the speaker our love for them, but the speaker will recognize we are good listeners and feel comfortable to divulge more about themselves with us.[125] Neither Gudykunst, Dodd, nor Elmer references each other on the topic of being a "good listener."

Gudykunst and Young Yun Kim explain the significance of being empathetic towards others.[126] The authors write, "When we are empathetic, we imagine how strangers are feeling."[127] Dodd describes that to empathetically communicate cross-culturally we should avoid: "sarcasm, fear, condescending messages, and controlling messages."[128] In Elmer's list of "Ten General Rules for Dealing with Conflict," he notes the importance of putting oneself in another's place and "appreciating their perspective."[129] Scott Moreau, Campbell, and Greener summarize Elmer's words as "empathy."[130] Elsewhere, Moreau, Campbell, and Greener mention Ted Ward's usage of "empathy," and how it involves "emotional connection, understanding the host worldview, and the ability to frame the actions of others in ways that make sense to them rather than ways that make sense to you."[131]

Also agreed on by the scholars is the significance of avoiding an ethnocentric attitude. Gudykunst and Hammer note how we cannot comprehend the host culture and people if we have an ethnocentric mindset.[132] Lustig and

---

121. Gudykunst, *Bridging Differences*, 184–85.
122. Dodd, *Dynamics of Intercultural Communication*, 202–3.
123. Dodd, *Dynamics of Intercultural Communication*, 202.
124. Dodd, *Dynamics of Intercultural Communication*, 203.
125. Elmer, *Cross-Cultural Servanthood*, 122.
126. Gudykunst and Kim, *Communicating with Strangers*, 289–90.
127. Gudykunst and Kim, *Communicating with Strangers*, 289.
128. Dodd, *Dynamics of Intercultural Communication*, 193.
129. Elmer, *Cross-Cultural Conflict*, 180–81.
130. Moreau et al., *Effective Intercultural Communication*, 346.
131. Moreau et al., *Effective Intercultural Communication*, 221.
132. Gudykunst and Hammer, "Strangers and Hosts," 116.

Koester write how ethnocentrism causes us to "highlight and exaggerate cultural differences."[133] We are to contemplate how our "emotional reactions" to "sights, sounds, and smells" in other cultures may reveal our own ethnocentric mindset.[134] In covering "ethnocentrism," Dodd references Gudykunst and Kim's (*Communicating with Strangers*) description of how ethnocentrism and prejudice lead to less effective communication.[135] Elmer also writes about "ethnocentrism," describing it more fully: it is the attitude that one's own culture and customs are superior to another culture's.[136] He adds that our ethnocentrism is obvious when we "resist change."[137] All other cultures are judged according to the standard of our own culture and group.[138]

Gudykunst and Kim express that, in order to build cross-cultural friendships, we are to avoid "negative stereotyping" them.[139] In another work, Gudykunst and Sudweeks note how we can understand those in other cultures only if we have correct "stereotypes" about them and their culture.[140] According to Lustig and Koester, if we have "faulty and inflexible stereotypes" about others, it will cause us to have prejudice feelings towards them.[141] We must recognize our own prejudice thinking in order to avoid having negative stereotypes of others. We can make a list of and be aware of positive and negative stereotypes and "ethnocentric attitudes about [outsiders'] appearances, foods, and social practices."[142] Elmer describes how, through learning from others, we can remove our and their stereotypes.[143] Moreau, Campbell, and Greener add that relationships are hindered because of "stereotypes."[144] To avoid this, we are to recognize the others as different than us rather than "one of us."[145]

---

133. Lustig and Koester, *Intercultural Competence*, 159.
134. Lustig and Koester, *Intercultural Competence*, 160.
135. Dodd, "Introduction," 6.
136. Elmer, *Cross-Cultural Servanthood*, 68.
137. Elmer, *Cross-Cultural Servanthood*, 132.
138. Elmer, *Cross-Cultural Servanthood*, 132.
139. Gudykunst and Kim, *Communicating with Strangers*, 346.
140. Gudykunst and Sudweeks, "Applying a Theory," 358.
141. Lustig and Koester, *Intercultural Competence*, 164.
142. Lustig and Koester, *Intercultural Competence*, 169.
143. Elmer, *Cross-Cultural Servanthood*, 98.
144. Moreau et al., *Effective Intercultural Communication*, 244.
145. Moreau et al., *Effective Intercultural Communication*, 244.

When building relationships cross-culturally, one must be willing to "self-disclose" with others about oneself. When discussing "self-disclosure," Gudykunst and Kim note how each culture has varying ideas on what people disclose to their friends.[146] Intercultural interactions are characterized by less self-disclosure than in-group interactions.[147] Lustig and Koester clarify how self-disclosure occurs more within friendships than between strangers or acquaintances.[148] For example, generally speaking, Japanese have many private matters they do not tell anyone, while Americans tend to share much about themselves.[149] Cultures all vary in the "breadth, depth, timing, and target" of self-disclosure.[150] Dodd writes how ideas about being "open" and "sharing" with others vary from culture to culture.[151] In general, high-context cultures have less self-disclosure. If one "under-discloses" in a culture that expects "high-disclosure," or one "over-discloses" in a context that values "low-disclosure," then "cultural conflict" ensues.[152] Elmer fails to directly mention "self-disclosure" in his writing; however, he does express how missionaries struggled to grow closer to the hosts because the missionaries were not open about their own struggles and sins.[153]

The scholars are in agreement concerning the need to develop a mastery of the host culture. Gudykunst and Kim explain "knowledge" and how it relates to knowing the other culture including differences and similarities between them and us.[154] We are to "be mindful" and recognize the other's perspective and not just our own.[155] For Lustig and Koester, "knowledge" is to possess an insight into the indigenous people. Culture-general knowledge is related to knowledge about general differences between cultures. But culture-specific knowledge is also necessary, to know how that particular culture is unique and its characteristics and customs.[156] Moreau, Campbell, and Greener also describe the distinction between culture-general

---

146. Gudykunst and Kim, *Communicating with Strangers*, 333.
147. Gudykunst and Kim, *Communicating with Strangers*, 344.
148. Lustig and Koester, *Intercultural Competence*, 227.
149. Lustig and Koester, *Intercultural Competence*, 244.
150. Lustig and Koester, *Intercultural Competence*, 244–45.
151. Dodd, *Dynamics of Intercultural Communication*, 189.
152. Dodd, *Dynamics of Intercultural Communication*, 190.
153. Elmer, *Cross-Cultural Conflict*, 157.
154. Gudykunst and Kim, *Communicating with Strangers*, 280–82.
155. Gudykunst and Kim, *Communicating with Strangers*, 283.
156. Lustig and Koester, *Intercultural Competence*, 69–70.

and culture-specific knowledge, although they do not explicitly reference Lustig and Koester.[157] Moreau, Campbell, and Greener write how culture-specific knowledge is necessary, and people must comprehend what needs to be known to "successfully navigate their daily lives" in the intercultural setting.[158] Elmer distinguishes between learning *about* and learning *from* others.[159] Learning *about* others is related to the knowledge we learn about the place before we arrive there.[160] When we are learning *from* others, we ask them questions and "probe their thoughts," that we may grasp their lives and culture.[161] We display a humble spirit to them and honor them by letting them teach us about their world.[162]

Gudykunst and Christian scholars are in agreement on the importance of learning the local language as well as blending in with the people in some ways by following the behaviors and customs of their culture. Gudykunst in multiple works mentions how we are to be flexible in our behavior and adapt to the behavior of strangers.[163] Likewise, one of Gudykunst and Hammer's axioms (# 23) is how learning the peoples' language facilitates us in appreciating their culture.[164] Lingenfelter and Mayers emphasize the necessity of missionaries being closely connected to the foreign culture; this is how the love of Christ is shown to the people.[165] Lingenfelter and Mayers endorse becoming what they term a "150 percent person," which includes learning what is central to those in the foreign context, following their values and rules, and understanding what characterizes and constitutes their lives, all with the goal of successfully building tight bonds with them.[166] All Christian resources reviewed agreed that it is important for missionaries to learn the host language well.[167]

---

157. Moreau et al., *Effective Intercultural Communication*, 232–33.

158. Moreau et al., *Effective Intercultural Communication*, 233.

159. Elmer, *Cross-Cultural Servanthood*, 93–99.

160. Elmer, *Cross-Cultural Servanthood*, 93–94.

161. Elmer, *Cross-Cultural Servanthood*, 97.

162. Elmer, *Cross-Cultural Servanthood*, 98.

163. Gudykunst and Kim, *Communicating with Strangers*, 292; Gudykunst and Sudweeks, "Applying a Theory," 365–66.

164. Gudykunst and Hammer, "Strangers and Hosts," 126.

165. Lingenfelter and Mayers, *Ministering Cross-Culturally*, 10–11.

166. Lingenfelter and Mayers, *Ministering Cross-Culturally*, 114.

167. Lingenfelter and Mayers, *Ministering Cross-Culturally*, 17; Moreau et al., *Effective Intercultural Communication*, 77–78; Elmer, *Cross-Cultural Servanthood*, 66, 77–78.

Missionary Attrition

Missionary attrition, as previously mentioned, relates to "acceptable" or "preventable" reasons why missionaries leave the mission field, with a particular focus on further minimizing "preventable" attrition. This is a relevant subject to study for this research, as the research investigates partly what contributes to retention for Chinese missionaries. In researching attrition for other missionaries from around the world (especially those from other "NSC" contexts), the Chinese missionaries' experiences for what contributes to their retention can be compared with the experiences of missionaries worldwide.

When analyzing missionary attrition literature, the 1997 William Taylor edited book *Too Valuable to Lose,* provided insights from several contributors. Rodolfo Giron writes on how the "best missionary" is one who understands the Bible well, grasps the role of the church, and who relates well with indigenous people and treats them with respect.[168] Kath Donovan and Ruth Myors note the critical nature of rigorously learning the host language for a period in the foreign land upon arrival.[169] Missionary attrition, in contrast, may arise when missionaries fail to connect with members of the host or do not show grace towards them.[170]

On the topic of attrition for NSC missionaries, one study found that Korean missionaries' primary attrition causes were: conflict between older and younger missionaries (16.5 percent), having health problems (13 percent), or changing jobs (13 percent).[171] Korean missionaries, as a result of their "monocultural" background, sometimes have difficulties in "cultural adaptation."[172] The Brazilian mission movement, however, was hindered primarily by a "lack of financial support," which was affected by Brazil's economic strain in the 1980s and '90s.[173] Within Brazil, the older the mission agency was, the fewer attrition problems they had.[174] Those

---

168. Giron, "Integrated Model of Missions," 34.
169. Donovan and Myors, "Reflections on Attrition in Career Missionaries," 58.
170. Platt, "Call to Partnership," 203.
171. Moon, "Missionary Attrition in Korea," 136.
172. Moon, "Missionary Attrition in Korea," 137.
173. Limpic, "Brazilian Missionaries," 149.
174. Limpic, "Brazilian Missionaries," 150.

ministering cross-culturally in contexts distant from Brazil had a higher level of attrition.[175]

For Ghanaian missions, 36 percent of missionaries returning home did so because of "personal problems" such as "immature spiritual life," low commitment level or low self-esteem, stress overload, pressures of singlehood, or want of a missionary call.[176] About 4 percent of Ghanaian mission attrition occurred because of an inability to learn the local language well or interact well with the people there.[177] Proud people struggle as missionaries, as do those who come from a "monocultural" culture.[178] More people fail in NSC missions because of an inability to grasp "leadership" and "followership" than because of theological reasons.

Missionaries from Africa may have a lack of exposure to the world beyond their immediate experience and thus have a "narrow worldview."[179] In addition, paramount for missionary retention, particularly with battling spiritual warfare in a foreign context, is persevering in "spiritual disciplines" like "prayer, Scripture memory, meditation, and fasting."[180]

An additional critical edited book about attrition has been the findings of the second WEA research project on attrition, ReMAP II, which was edited by Rob Hay and published in 2007. Both ReMAP and ReMAP II findings were based on empirical research, in the form of interviews and case studies. Rob Hay mentions how mission agencies with high retention have twice as many missionaries with master's and doctorate degrees.[181] Though generally speaking missionaries with higher levels of formal school education are more effective on the field, in the same section of the book, Jaap Ketelaar also gives examples of people with less formal education who have been effective in missions.[182] Nathaniel Abimbola explains how missionaries with his mission in Nigeria lack formal school education beyond primary or middle school, but "[they] have not seen any adverse results in ministry outcomes on the field as a result

---

175. Limpic, "Brazilian Missionaries," 151.
176. Anyomi, "Attrition in Ghana," 165.
177. Anyomi, "Attrition in Ghana," 166.
178. Taylor, "Challenging the Missions Stakeholders," 358.
179. Anyomi, "Mission Agency Screening," 231.
180. Anyomi, "Mission Agency Screening," 234.
181. Hay, "Education," 55.
182. Ketelaar, "Education," 58.

of low education."[183] Later in the book, Ketelaar explains the necessity of missionaries having a robust spiritual life.[184] Amidst the pressures of missionary work, missionaries have to be consistent in having time with Jesus, studying the Bible, and praying.[185]

In the same book, it is explained how family blessing is vital for the retention of NSC missionaries. Sarah Hay writes, "The blessing of family increases a missionary's likelihood of staying on the field for NSC missionaries. In cultures where filial piety is important, family blessing has a significant impact on whether missionary candidates can fulfill their call."[186] Vanessa Hung describes how filial piety is a major virtue in the Chinese context.[187] It is expected that Chinese children take care of their aging parents. This obligation to take care of their parents can hinder Chinese from going on the mission field. Hung explains how churches in China could aid Chinese missionaries by caring for the parents of the Chinese missionaries. This would facilitate the Chinese missionaries freely ministering in a foreign land without feeling guilty of abandoning their parents.[188] Later in the same book, Korean Dong-Hwa Kim describes how, in non-Western countries, a system to provide for senior citizens is lacking.[189] These elderly are taken care of by their children. Thus, those in the home country can serve their missionary families by regularly calling and visiting their missionaries' parents as well as organizing events where missionary parents can meet one another.[190]

On the topic of single missionaries, Sarah Hay explains how missionaries must be content about their marital status.[191] Since peoples' weaknesses and insecurities are magnified when moving to a new culture, insecurities about singlehood may develop into depression, ineffectiveness in ministry, and interpersonal conflict with others. Later in the same book, Meer explains how single missionaries need special pastoral care. They often struggle with loneliness and need assistance in finding their role in their teams, that they

183. Abimbola, "Is Higher Education Required," 62.
184. Ketelaar, "Spiritual Life," 132.
185. Ketelaar, "Spiritual Life," 134.
186. Hay, "Selection: What it Means," 71.
187. Hung, "Filial Piety and Missionary Calling," 78.
188. Hung, "Filial Piety and Missionary Calling," 78.
189. Kim, "Ministry to the Elderly Parents of Missionaries," 366.
190. Kim, "Ministry to the Elderly Parents of Missionaries," 366.
191. Hay, "Selection: What it Means," 73.

may be seen as contributors and respected by teammates.[192] In the book *Global Mission Handbook*, the anonymous author Peter's wife expressed how single women on the mission field face unique challenges since they fail to receive relational benefits that come through marriage.[193] A way to aid these women is to provide mentors who will care for them as well as help them with practical needs such as support raising. Common challenges for these women are: "wondering if they would ever marry, loneliness, not having a sounding board, and concerns about how to develop close relationships with other women."[194] Some single women missionaries feared for their safety. In addition to maintaining regular communication with these single missionaries, it is also imperative for someone to regularly visit them or at least ship a "care package" to them.[195]

In *Worth Keeping*, Rob Hay explains how a calling from God is prevalent for inspiring people to go to the mission field.[196] Additionally, it is essential for NSC missionaries that their home church and pastor endorse them.[197] It is also important that they receive strong practical and administrative on-field support from their mission agency.[198] Lack of medical insurance contributes to NSC missionary attrition: if they have medical difficulties, they may need to return to their home country for care.[199]

Detlef Blocher explained how ReMAP revealed that a close relationship with teammates is one of the four primary reasons given by missionaries for staying on the field.[200] Imperative for NSC missionaries is having effective teams, pastoral care on the field, and interpersonal conflict resolution.[201] Because NSCs are often community-oriented, "effectiveness in teams is linked much more strongly with retention."[202] This research also revealed that NCS missionaries are more effective in interpersonal conflict resolution than were the Western missionaries researched, potentially because of the

192. Meer, "Personal Care of Our Missionaries," 154.
193. Peter's Wife, "Challenges of Single Women," 175.
194. Peter's Wife, "Challenges of Single Women," 175.
195. Peter's Wife, "Challenges of Single Women," 175–76.
196. Hay, "Selection—Calling and Tested Call," 94.
197. Hay, "Selection—Calling and Tested Call," 95.
198. Hay, "Personal Care: What it Means," 151.
199. Hay, "Personal Care: What it Means," 153.
200. Blocher, "ReMAP I," 15.
201. Hay, "Personal Care: What it Means", 150.
202. Hay, "Personal Care—Team Building and Functioning", 163.

relational cultures they originated from.[203] However, tension and conflict within a team can be a distraction and burden for those missionaries.[204] Rob Hay described the heightened challenges for missionaries on multicultural teams: "[Intercultural] teams are challenging because people struggle with difference. Conflict in multicultural teams may be interpreted through cultural terms or caused by cultural difference."[205]

Also pertinent is caring for the missionaries. In the same book, Antonia Leonora van der Meer explains how Brazilian mission agencies are now putting more emphasis on member care, though in the previous decades these agencies failed in caring for their missionaries.[206] Likewise, Rob Hay notes that ReMAP II has confirmed the significance of effective member care for NSC missionaries' retention.[207] Detlef Blocher explains that member care includes: "pastoral care, personal encouragement, team building, spiritual refreshment, and professional counseling in critical incidents."[208] ReMAP I revealed how effective missionary care results in greater missionary retention.[209] The higher retaining mission agencies invested twice the finances in member care, thus producing a superior organizational culture of missionary care. Additionally, "effective communication" between the missionary and the mission agency leads to higher retention of missionaries.[210] Neal Pirolo describes how a set person in the mission agency or home church needs to regularly correspond with the missionary.[211]

On the topic of finances, as previously mentioned, "sustainable finances" was listed by Howard Brant as the largest hindrance for majority world missions.[212] Korean, Brazilian, African, and Indian mission movements have all, at some point, been hampered by a shortage of finances.[213]

---

203. Hay, "Personal Care—Team Building and Functioning: What it Means," 165.

204. Hay, "Personal Care—Conflict and Teams," 175.

205. Hay, "Personal Care—Conflict and Team What it Means," 176.

206. Meer, "Personal Care of Our Missionaries," 153.

207. Hay, "Member Care," 181–82.

208. Blocher, "Member Care," 182.

209. Blocher, "Member Care," 183.

210. Hay, "Home Office," 362.

211. Pirolo, "Raising the Standard for Missionary Care," 173.

212. Brant, "Seven Essentials," 50.

213. Korean (Cho, "Diagnostic Survey of Missionary Movements," 92); Brazilian (Limpic, "Brazilian Missionaries," 149); African (Turaki, "Evangelical Missiology from Africa," 281); and, Indian (Rajendran, "Emergence and Expansion of Indian Mission," 73.

However, the Korean movement has been aided in recent decades by Korean economic development, which has allowed for more sending of Korean missionaries.[214]

Rob Hay noted that mission agencies that provide steady financial support have higher retention of missionaries.[215] Valerie Lim lists how overlooked financial costs relevant to missionaries include: children's education, insurance coverage (for health, life, property, or evacuation), and retirement funds.[216] Denis Lane adds that it is imperative to have an understanding of what exactly the mission agency will or will not pay for, such as children's education, medical expenses, transportation costs, or retirement funding.[217] Lim explains how NSC missionaries without a financial backup may sometimes have their financial support cut off and need to make adjustments in order to remain on the mission field.[218] Similarly, Blocher adds how it is essential for NSC missionaries to have financial backup if they are in a situation of having low finances.[219] Philip Chang suggests overcoming low financial support by sending "tentmakers" that work full-time on the mission field.[220] Chang mentions Ah Kie Lim's example of how "income-generating strategies" on the mission field provided an income when financial support from the home country was low[221]. Lane also emphasizes that missionaries should know before they leave how their financial needs will be met, as Paul knew during his missionary journeys he could earn money through making tents.[222] Lane added that an additional difficulty faced is that some home country currencies may be harder to exchange on the mission field than the US dollar.[223]

Frank Allen noted that missionaries may return home because of "culture shock" and hating the host culture.[224] The article does not appear to be

---

214. Moon, *Korean Missionary Movement*, 6–7; Park, "Missionary Movement of the Korean Church," 167–69.

215. Hay, "Finances," 339.

216. Lim, "Finances," 341.

217. Lane, *Tuning God's New Instruments*, 55.

218. Lim, "Finances," 342.

219. Blocher, "Good Agency Practices," 233.

220. Chang, "Overcoming Low Financial Support," 354.

221. Chang, "Overcoming Low Financial Support," 356.

222. Lane, *Tuning God's New Instruments*, 52.

223. Lane, *Tuning God's New Instruments*, 54.

224. Allen, "Why Do They Leave?," 119.

PRECEDENT LITERATURE

based on empirical evidence, but rather on conversations with people in his organization. Sometimes husbands may neglect their family because of their commitment to the ministry, which overburdens the family.[225]. Other missionaries have disagreements with, or failed expectations towards, their mission agency leaders. Missionaries may also leave the mission field because of a failure to learn the new language.[226]

Allan D. Stirling, in his PhD dissertation on missionary attrition, conducted his empirical research by interviewing missionaries from the U.S.[227] Stirling notes that the largest contingent of "preventable causes of attrition" was missionary disagreements with the mission agency leadership in the U.S. "Loneliness and isolation" also led to some missionaries leaving the field.[228] Other missionaries described how cross-cultural adaptation problems led to their departure.[229] Usually, attrition was "multi-faceted" and had multiple factors; furthermore, "preventable and unpreventable factors" often combined.[230] However, most issues for attrition were "preventable."[231]

Hark Yoo Kim in his dissertation about missionary attrition of majority world missionaries, wrote about Korean missionaries serving in Japan. He found that one aspect of missionary retention was having a strong call to reach the Japanese.[232] Several Korean missionaries had left the field because of feelings of resentment towards Japan.[233] Maintaining a consistent devotional life was critical for retention.[234] Cross-cultural training was helpful for the interviewees, as was host language proficiency and competency in the Japanese culture and society.[235] Building credibility in the Japanese culture is paramount and takes time.[236] For Korean missionaries, another influence for retention is having friendly relationships with other

---

225. Allen, "Why Do They Leave?" 121.
226. Allen, "Why Do They Leave?" 121–22.
227. Stirling, "Missionary Attrition among Missionaries," 102.
228. Stirling, "Missionary Attrition among Missionaries," 103.
229. Stirling, "Missionary Attrition among Missionaries," 104.
230. Stirling, "Missionary Attrition among Missionaries," 106.
231. Stirling, "Missionary Attrition among Missionaries," 107.
232. Kim, "Retention Factors among Korean Missionaries," 62.
233. Kim, "Retention Factors among Korean Missionaries," 69.
234. Kim, "Retention Factors among Korean Missionaries," 74.
235. Kim, "Retention Factors among Korean Missionaries," 77, 96, 117.
236. Kim, "Retention Factors among Korean Missionaries," 121.

missionaries.²³⁷ Some Korean missionaries had left the mission field because of the wife's culture shock and burnout.²³⁸

Missionary Training

Some authors emphasize the importance of having pre-field cross-cultural experience. An influential multi-authored book about missionary training is the *Global Mission Handbook*, which was published in 2009 and edited by William D. Taylor and Steve Hoke. This work explains that people fail to understand their own culture until they experience another culture, which gives them a new perspective.²³⁹ Thus, it is beneficial in missionary preparation to experience cross-cultural living. Only when we experience different cultures do we realize the immense differences between various cultures and ours. Though some are naturally gifted in crossing cultures, it is essential for all to "deliberately broaden their exposure to other cultures."²⁴⁰ Highly suggested is having numerous cross-cultural opportunities, to be truly "tested." Taking a short-term mission trip may be advantageous, but it is noted that ample cross-cultural opportunities also exist within one's own country. The authors conclude, "[Having cross-cultural experiences] will sharpen your sense of the delightful differences between cultures and heighten your awareness of the need to build bridges."²⁴¹ In Evelyn Hibbert's book *Training Missionaries*, she stresses the necessity of learning about other cultures by personally experiencing them for an ample amount of time.²⁴² This leads to people fighting against their ethnocentric tendencies.

Multiple authors stress the correlation between missionary training and missionary retention. In Rob Hay's edited book about WEA's second attrition study ReMAP II, *Worth Keeping*, Detlef Blocher explains how the data reveals that missionaries who receive longer periods of training generally stay longer on the mission field; those who have at least a year of missionary training stay twice as long on the field as those who do not.²⁴³ Rob Hay describes how

---

237. Kim, "Retention Factors among Korean Missionaries," 162.
238. Kim, "Retention Factors among Korean Missionaries," 179.
239. Hoke and Taylor, "Exposure to Other Cultures," 107.
240. Hoke and Taylor, "Exposure to Other Cultures," 107.
241. Hoke and Taylor, "Exposure to Other Cultures," 107.
242. Hibbert, *Training Missionaries*, 69.
243. Blocher, "ReMAP I," 18.

agencies with high retention require twice as much theological education.[244] William Taylor adds that one of the main causes of preventable missionary attrition is a lack of proper training and learning to prepare them for their ministry.[245] *Too Valuable to Lose*, the edited book about the first attrition research done by WEA, also emphasizes how superior training results in less attrition. Noted is that 4.5 percent of NSC attrition was related to "insufficient training."[246] Blocher and Lewis explain that mission agencies with lower attrition give priority to missiology, theology, and cross-cultural training: "Generally, more training means less attrition."[247]

Numerous authors emphasize the necessity of missionaries receiving pre-field missiological training. Detlef Blocher clarifies how mission agencies with lower missionary attrition had higher standards for missiological training.[248] Rob Hay further expounds on this, saying that agencies with higher missionary retention have two or three times "higher minimal requirement in formal missiological training."[249] Hay describes pre-field missiological training as the most beneficial training for missionary retention.[250] Writing on this topic, Jonathan Ingleby adds how mission agencies should strongly consider how missiological training is "more effective preparation" than training in a Bible school.[251] Noted by Ingleby is the phenomenon of missionaries, even after receiving formal biblical training, lacking an understanding of how their Bibles connect to life on the mission field. Mission training should be "mission focused, cross-cultural, and practical" (involving "experiential learning").[252] Ekstrom adds elsewhere how young people who are interested in missions but lack international experience should receive pre-field cross-cultural and missiological training.[253]

In *Global Mission Handbook*, the editors note the importance of a strong foundation in the Bible, as it is the Bible that "establishes [our] faith,

---

244. Hay, "Preparation Time," 106.
245. Taylor, "What about Missionary Attrition?," 269.
246. Brierley, "Missionary Attrition," 94.
247. Blocher and Lewis, "Further Findings in the Research Data," 118.
248. Blocher, "ReMAP I," 18.
249. Hay, "Education," 55.
250. Hay, "Preparation Time," 107.
251. Ingleby, "Preparation Time," 107.
252. Ingleby, "Preparation Time," 108.
253. Ekstrom, "Selection Process and the Issue of Attrition," 189.

undergirds [our] values, [and] guides [our] behavior and ministry."[254] The editors recommend not only having an adequate missiological and theological education, but also receiving training in the social sciences, and having language and culture learning training.[255]

In Hibbert's book *Training Missionaries*, she suggests that a beneficial method for missionary preparation is to read missionary biographies.[256] These biographies are useful for gaining an understanding of the task of ministering cross-culturally. However, countless missionaries leave for the field without having any exposure to past missionaries' experiences. Thus, they often make similar mistakes, ones that have been repeated for centuries.[257]

As for missionary training resources pertaining to cross-cultural training of Asian missionaries, David Tai-Woong Lee in 2008 wrote an article in the journal *Missiology*. Lee explains how missionaries from monocultural Asian contexts (Korea, China, Japan) are ill-prepared to "meet the challenges of globalization."[258] Lee explains how such missionaries are devoid of the "character building that enables them to cope with different cultural values in multicultural situations."[259] A training program in Korea GMTC is designed specifically for missionaries from a monocultural background.

Lee describes how it can be beneficial for those from monocultural backgrounds to be in a multicultural context.[260] Sometimes doing this can facilitate that person developing personal character, cross-cultural ministry skills, and missiological learning. But other times, such a person being in this multicultural context can become even more closed to others and experience an increased feeling of ethnocentrism. Missionaries from monocultural contexts must develop sensitivity in interacting with other cultures, as they may interact on the mission field with not only hosts there but also with other missionaries from around the world. Later these missionaries from Asia will also need cultural sensitivity if they desire to work alongside the host church and other Christians in that country.[261]

254. Hoke and Taylor, "Hands-On Missionary Training," 208–9.
255. Hoke and Taylor, "Hands-On Missionary Training," 209–10.
256. Hibbert, *Training Missionaries*, 56.
257. Hibbert, *Training Missionaries*, 56.
258. Lee, "Training Cross-Cultural Missionaries," 112.
259. Lee, "Training Cross-Cultural Missionaries," 112.
260. Lee, "Training Cross-Cultural Missionaries," 113.
261. Lee, "Training Cross-Cultural Missionaries," 114.

Lee mentions nine objectives stressed by the Evangelical Fellowship of Asia Mission Commission missionary trainers' consultation held in 1993 in Manila.²⁶² These are: spiritual maturity; integrity of character; stable family life; resilience in emotional and physical health; relational skills; basics in biblical and theological knowledge; understanding missiology; cross-cultural ministry skills; and practical life skills. Lee describes GMTC's missionary training as involving learning "the meaning of culture; how to cope with and overcome culture shock; methods for language acquisition; how to communicate in different cultures; how to minister in cross-cultural situations and cope with stress in a different culture; theological issues in going into a cross-cultural situation; and the biblical and theological basis of cross-cultural mission."²⁶³

On the topic of training Asian missionaries, Titus Loong describes the unique challenges of Asian missionaries including the necessity of having to learn English.²⁶⁴ He writes, "We have to adjust to two new languages and two new cultures. We must study the target language as well as English, and learn to adjust to the indigenous culture as well as the 'missionary culture' that dominates in missionary gatherings."²⁶⁵ Seth Anyomi adds how missionaries from the "two-thirds world," which includes Asia, benefit from having pre-field training on vocational development, that they may have an occupation on the mission field.²⁶⁶

Church in China

Varying estimates exist as to the number of Christians in China. Conservative estimates are 50 million and 60 million.²⁶⁷ Lian Xi explains how China had only 80,000 Christians in 1900 in a land of 400 million. But now China has tens of millions of Christians, over 600 times the amount in 1900.²⁶⁸

Rodney Stark and Wang Xiuhua write of the prevalence of Christians in rural contexts. They note how in some rural areas of China, Christianity is widespread. In 2007 5.3 percent of people in Henan Province, which

262. Lee, "Training Cross-Cultural Missionaries," 116.
263. Lee, "Training Cross-Cultural Missionaries," 117.
264. Loong, "Training Missionaries in Asia," 44.
265. Loong, "Training Missionaries in Asia," 44.
266. Anyomi, "Mission Agency Screening," 236.
267. Xi, *Redeemed by Fire*, 2; Stark and Wang, *Star in the East*, 11.
268. Xi, *Redeemed by Fire*, 2.

is two-thirds rural, were Christians.[269] In a 2012 study in Funan County, part of the heavily Christian and agricultural Anhui Province, 32 percent of the population identified themselves as Christians.[270] In this same county, three-fourths of the professed Christians regularly read their Bibles. More than half of the professed Christians, including six Communist Party members, said they regularly share their faith with others.[271] Tony Lambert writes of large house church networks in the mostly rural provinces of Henan and Anhui.[272] Most of these house churches are in rural areas and the congregants and pastors often lack education beyond elementary school or middle school. For the last thirty years, each of these house church networks has been sending their people all around China to plant churches, thus sizeable national networks have formed.[273]

Fenggang Yang describes the pervasiveness of young and educated Christians in Chinese cities.[274] Over 50 percent of believers in a city in southern China were between the ages of 18 and 39. In a study of Christians in Shanghai conducted in 1980, 15 percent of believers were under 40 years old. By 1990, 27 percent were under 40 years old.[275] Brent Fulton elaborates on this phenomenon of the growth of educated and "young to middle-aged" urban Christian professionals.[276] Numerous intellectuals became open to the Christian faith after the government's crushing of the 1989 Tiananmen Square demonstrations and then became outspoken Christians from inside or outside China. Goossaert and Palmer write of urban Christians in China. They explain that, contrary to the perception that Christians in China were only elderly and poor rural residents, it became obvious in the late 1990s that many educated and wealthy young urbanites were becoming Christians.[277] College students at the prestigious university Renmin University in Beijing completed a survey.[278] Though only 3.2 percent of those surveyed said they were Christians, 61.5 percent of them expressed an

269. Stark and Wang, *Star in the East*, 91.
270. Stark and Wang, *Star in the East*, 96.
271. Stark and Wang, *Star in the East*, 97.
272. Lambert, *China's Christian Millions*, 65.
273. Lambert, *China's Christian Millions*, 65.
274. Yang, "Lost in the Market, Saved at McDonald's," 429.
275. Yang, "Lost in the Market, Saved at McDonald's," 428.
276. Fulton, *China's Urban Christians*, 10.
277. Goossaert and Palmer, *Religious Question in Modern China*, 301–2.
278. Goossaert and Palmer, *Religious Question in Modern China*, 302.

"interest" in Christianity. Though an abundance of wealthy and educated Chinese Christians exert influence in their respective professional fields, Lian Xi explains how Christianity in China has been and will continue to be "primarily a religion of the masses, far from the center of political power," uninvolved in political activism or appeals for social justice.[279]

Brent Fulton describes the two divisions of churches in China: those in the legal government-registered Three-Self Patriotic Movement (TSPM), and those in the unregistered and illegal house churches.[280] Fulton explains that all TSPM churches do not necessarily have liberal theology and collude with the government, as is often perceived. The widespread perception of all "real Christians" being in doctrinally sound house churches is erroneous. Some TSPM churches are evangelistic and some house churches are heretical. On the topic of demarcations within Chinese churches, Tony Lambert notes that in China the churches are void of any denominational boundaries similar to what exists in the West.[281]

Concerning the background of Christianity (and other religious practices) in China over the course of the last 70 years, Yao explains that for the majority of the second half of the twentieth century, beginning with Chairman Mao's leadership, religions were suppressed to varying degrees, particularly from the 1950s through the 1970s.[282] Beginning in the 1980s, however, all forms of religion in China, including Christianity, have flourished, which continues until today. Ian Johnson adds that in 1982 the Chinese Communist Party (CCP) produced a document on religious freedom that legalized at home or in worship places "Buddha worship, scripture chanting, incense burning, prayer, Bible study, preaching, Mass, baptism, initiation as a monk or a nun, fasting, and celebrations of religious festivals."[283]

The Contribution of This Study

Prior studies have failed to use the aforementioned concepts to examine the experiences of Chinese missionaries, including their retention in missionary service. The precedent literature does not reveal studies about the

279. Xi, *Redeemed by Fire*, 242.
280. Fulton, "China," 177.
281. Lambert, *China's Christian Millions*, 58–59.
282. Yao, *Religious Experience in Contemporary China*, 6.
283. Johnson, *Souls of China*, 28.

phenomenon of Chinese missionary sending in general, or the attrition and retention of such missionaries in particular. As the Chinese mission movement has yet to be previously empirically researched, all aspects of this study are, thus, new contributions to the literature on Chinese missions.

This study will provide an initial qualitative investigation into factors contributing to intercultural adjustment, preparation, and retention of Chinese missionaries. Attention will be given to unique challenges faced by Chinese missionaries.

3

Research Methodology

THIS CHAPTER IS AN account of the methodological approach utilized in the research. It will first explain why the dissertation used qualitative research. Second it will describe the sampling procedures, instrumentation, data collection, and data analysis. Finally it will address validity, reliability, biases, and permissions.

Qualitative narrative interviews were conducted, which are semi-structured, short-story, and life-story. Qualitative research is ideal in many regards for this dissertation. I researched the Chinese missionaries' personal experiences on the mission field. Qualitative research interview "gives a privileged access to people's basic experience of the lived world."[1] Additionally, this topic of Chinese missionaries is almost completely unexplored. Qualitative research leads to key discoveries being made in an unknown field.[2] A qualitative research approach allows the experiences of the Chinese missionaries to shape the research. This leads to obtaining access to profounder experiences of the subjects and complex dynamics.[3]

These interviews were narrative interviews that "center on the stories the subjects tell, [and] on the plots and structures of their accounts."[4] Narrative interviews facilitate obtaining stories that "inform us of the human world of meanings."[5] After the initial request for their story, interrupting them was avoided, but rather listening carefully to the duration of their story, and asking for clarifications when necessary.[6] In narrative interviews, the narrative "can refer to a specific episode or course of action significant

---

1. Kvale and Brinkmann, *Interviews*, 29.
2. Kvale and Brinkmann, *Interviews*, 83.
3. Kvale and Brinkmann, *Interviews*, 82.
4. Kvale and Brinkmann, *Interviews*, 153.
5. Kvale and Brinkmann, *Interviews*, 55.
6. Kvale and Brinkmann, *Interviews*, 155.

to the narrator, leading to a *short story*."[7] Narrative interviews were used in this research because narrative facilitates the interviewees telling concretely what happened to them. Their narratives were used to uncover unexpected responses. These interview questions were semi-structured. There was some flexibility in the topics discussed in the interview.[8]

The interviewees had a different home culture than the interviewer's. Difficulties exist in interviewing cross-culturally, and being "aware of the multitude of cultural factors that affect the relationship between interviewer and interviewee."[9] Thankfully, in this instance, I am familiar with the Chinese culture; I have lived in China ten years. I still needed to be aware of the cross-cultural communication differences, that in the communication in our interviews we had "different norms, . . . initiative, directness, [and] modes of questioning."[10]

Nonetheless, doing the interviews in a second language required more closely following the list of interview questions. The interviews were more structured and inflexible compared to doing the interviews in a first language. Open-ended questions and follow-up questions were asked to facilitate the interviewees telling personal stories. This being said, for the first few interviews the list of interview questions were more closely followed and few follow-up questions were asked. But after a few interviews, I learned how to improve the interview techniques, and felt more comfortable in listening to and following what the interviewees were saying. Then they could be asked follow-up questions. Also, by recording and later transcribing the interviews, and by using the narrative approach, researcher bias was reduced.

Informant Selection, Sampling Criteria, and Sampling Procedure

Those interviewed were all from Mainland China serving as a missionary outside of China and ministering among those from the non-Chinese host culture there. A scattered sample of Chinese missionaries was interviewed, representing numerous international or Chinese mission organizations. An email (see email at Appendix 4) was sent to about

7. Kvale and Brinkmann, *Interviews*, 155.
8. Kvale and Brinkmann, *Interviews*, 130.
9. Kvale and Brinkmann, *Interviews*, 144.
10. Kvale and Brinkmann, *Interviews*, 144.

sixty personal contacts that are connected to ministry in China and were thought to potentially have contacts to Chinese missionaries. They were asked if they knew any Chinese missionaries, or if they had other contacts connected to Chinese missionaries. Some of these people sent contact information for Chinese missionaries they knew. Others did not personally know Chinese missionaries, but they sent contacts of theirs who they thought were connected to Chinese missionaries. Then these contacts were emailed and asked if they had contact to any Chinese missionaries. Some of them introduced Chinese missionaries.

Additional contacts for the research were through a close acquaintance within one Chinese mission organization. Several of their missionaries were interviewed for this research.

Chinese missionaries were emailed a personal introduction and an introduction of the research (see Appendix 3). In this initial correspondence with them, they were asked to ensure that they met the research requirements: that they were connected to house churches in China, and that they had been cross-cultural missionaries outside China for at least two years working among non-Chinese people.

Three of the people interviewed were not incorporated into the research. Two of these people had become believers in the U.S., and had been sent by Chinese mission agencies in the U.S. They were without a background within house churches in China, which was one of the research requirements. The third person interviewed but excluded was someone who met all the necessary requirements initially, but through the interview, it was discovered that he was in fact not ministering to host non-Chinese in the foreign country, though in initial correspondence he had said he was. Also, a young woman introduced through another Chinese missionary was beginning to be interviewed, but when she was asked the background questions, it was determined she had only been on the mission field 1.5 years, rather than at least two years. I apologized to her and told her that the interview would be stopped and not used.

Initially it was intended to only interview Chinese missionaries sent through Chinese mission agencies. But after two weeks of receiving few responses from people who could assist in finding contacts that met these requirements, the research requirements were broadened to incorporate Chinese missionaries from Mainland China that belonged to international mission agencies. Of the 25 Chinese missionaries interviewed, approximately half belonged to international mission agencies.

Half were through Chinese mission agencies or independently through Chinese house churches.

Chinese missionaries were interviewed who have been on the field for a minimum of two years. A portion of the interviewees had been missionaries for five or ten or more years. By doing this, multiple perspectives were gained. A plausible assumption is that those who have served longer on the field generally flourish most cross-culturally. However, such people may poorly represent the majority of Chinese missionaries, as those who stay longer would usually be missionaries who have success in cross-cultural missions and adaptation. Missionaries who have been on the field for a shorter period were also interviewed; these would be ones who would more likely struggle cross-culturally, and return to China within two or three years. Only Chinese missionaries serving with a "long-term" mindset were interviewed, rather than anyone doing "short-term missions," in which they from the beginning had committed to only serve for a couple of years.

The primary method used for determining the sample was purposive sampling; the needs and purposes were determined and then those who fit those requirements were found.[11] In this instance, research subjects were long-term Chinese missionaries from Mainland China, who serve outside China, are ministering cross-culturally to reach non-Chinese on the mission field, and have been on the mission field at least two years. With these constraints, I have taken what is available to me that matched my research requirements.[12] The available population that fits these research requirements is small. Because of the oppressive Chinese government, these Chinese missionaries must function covertly and not in the open.

Also used was "chain referral" sampling.[13] Those mission contacts that responded to my initial request were asked if they could introduce to me other people who have some connections within the Chinese mission community. When those Chinese missionaries introduced by contacts were contacted and they agreed to do the interview, they were asked if they knew any other Chinese missionaries to introduce. One Chinese missionary in Central Asia when first contacted introduced me to several other Chinese missionaries that she knew who lived in her country. After the Chinese missionaries were interviewed, they were asked if they knew other Chinese missionaries to introduce for the research. Many interviewed were met in

---

11. Bernard, *Research Methods in Anthropology*, 189.
12. Bernard, *Research Methods in Anthropology*, 190.
13. Bernard, *Research Methods in Anthropology*, 192–93.

this way. The first time Chinese missionaries were asked to introduce other Chinese missionaries they knew, many did not name any. Nevertheless, after completing the interview with them, when they were asked if they knew other Chinese missionaries they could introduce, some assisted by introducing other Chinese missionaries that could be interviewed.

Instrumentation, Data Collection, Recording Procedures, Transcribing, and Data Analysis

As the researcher, I was the primary instrument for data collection.[14] The questions were presented to the interviewees in a manner in which their trust could be gained, that they might be willing to openly disclose their experiences. A self-introduction helped establish their trust. Chinese missionaries, for security reasons, may be reluctant to participate in the research. Thus wherever possible I sought to obtain an introduction to the potential interviewee by a trusted Chinese leader or contact who could vouch for my trustworthiness. At the end of the interview with the Chinese missionaries, they were asked if they had any prayer requests. This question showed them that they were personally cared for, and that I was not simply interested in them because they were helping my research. They were told that I wanted to continue to keep in touch with them.

The missionaries knew that people from multiple mission organizations were interviewed; thus, they were more likely to openly communicate if they had any negative experiences, not fearing that their organization might "lose face." Questions were asked in a non-threatening way, that they might not get the impression they were being judged for their cross-cultural experiences. The purpose of the research was described to them, and they were asked background and casual conversation questions. Because the interviews were conducted online using the Internet media WhatsApp and Skype, the interviewees gave oral consent to the *Informed Consent Letter* (Appendix 2), which was read to them, and confidentiality and anonymity were explained.

Some of the Chinese missionaries interviewed live in countries where missionary activity is illegal. In some instances, if the government in that context is antagonistic against Christianity and missionaries, some potential interviewees may have been unable to participate for fear of their personal security and ministry. To alleviate such concern from missionaries, it

14. Kvale and Brinkmann, *Interviews*, 83.

was explained to them how interviews were recorded on my personal computer to help protect Chinese missionaries' security. All of this interview information has remained on my personal computer, and was not made publicly available. All audio recordings of the interviews will be deleted upon completion of the dissertation and its successful defense.

Twenty-five Chinese missionaries were interviewed. They were interviewed on WhatsApp or Skype, and the interviews were audio recorded. Interviewing online was most convenient; it was impractical and financially unfeasible to travel to interview all those missionaries serving in different countries. However, only using online interviews for the research and not using observational research methods resulted in limitations of the findings. For example, I was unable to observe how the subjects interact with hosts and thus could have obtained richer data. Using Mandarin Chinese, I personally interviewed all the research subjects. Though there were some linguistic problems understanding some of what the first few interviewees were saying, after a few interviews my listening of the interviewees improved and I felt more comfortable and confident with each interview. Most of what they said during the interview could be understood and their responses could be competently interacted with. Questions explored their experience building relationships and other experiences on the mission field.

During the interviews, several interviewees were reserved in sharing. When they were asked questions, they answered with one word or sentence. Even when they were asked for examples or further explanation, they still said little. Possibly this reservation was because they in general are quiet people and feel less comfortable talking to others. Or they may have distrusted the interviewer. Or they thought that their mission performance would be judged, and they felt insecure about their lives as a missionary. For some of them, it was perhaps their personality that generally is suspicious and closed to others. Though this was the case for some of the interviewees, for most of the interviews, after several minutes, they opened up and shared extensively about their experiences on the mission field. Several of the interviewees talked endlessly and were hard to guide in the interview. Those interviews were longer, and included talk about unrelated topics. Sometimes in such interviews not all of the interview questions could be asked. In such instances, they were still asked the most critical questions.

Another challenge was to keep track of exactly when the Chinese missionaries were interviewed. The reason this was a factor is that there may be up to seven or eight interviews within a given week, and all of the interviewees were living all around the world and in different time zones. For one interview, it was in the morning when I realized that I was supposed to have Skyped her an hour earlier and I had missed it. She was contacted and apologized to and she was asked if she could interview at that moment. She was gracious enough to oblige. After this situation, which occurred relatively early on in the interviews, more attention was put into who was being interviewed each day or week, and when they needed to be interviewed. There were no repeated similar incidents.

Technical difficulties existed. For some interviewees the Internet connection was weak, so they cut in and out. These cases were rare, and if they could not be clearly understood, they were asked to repeat what they just said. Some of the interviewees were hard to hear for other reasons. They spoke quickly or quietly or mumbled and were hard to understand. During one interview, screaming children were in the background of his home, which made it harder to understand. Another interviewee was standing outside at night during the interview, so crickets and other outside noises could be heard.

Some interview questions proved unhelpful. For example, Question 3.5 about how well they understand the host culture evoked responses that failed to reveal the interviewees' intercultural competence. It is possible that some who flourished cross-culturally said how little they understood about the culture, while those who seem to struggle cross-culturally responded that they had a strong understanding of the host culture. This was the only interview question for which all the responses were discarded.

After some interviews were completed, the audio recordings of the interviews were transcribed word for word in Chinese. At first, it took a couple full days of work to complete transcribing one interview. Some recordings needed to be slowly re-listened to many times before full sentences and paragraphs could be understood and transcribed. But after transcribing a few interviews, transcribing skills improved. Eventually an entire one-hour long interview could be transcribed in about six hours.

Sometimes, if after repeated listening to and trying to guess what they were saying, if there was still uncertainty about the meaning, a few question marks were written in the transcription to indicate that this section was a part that could not be understood. But these instances were few. In such instances those parts of the responses were not used as quotes in the analysis of the interviews or in NVivo. A Chinese friend whose first language is Chinese and is fluent in English helped by listening to ten-minute sections of three of the interviews, to ensure that the transcriptions and translations of the interviews were accurate. He confirmed their accuracy, and that minimal minor mistakes were made that did not negatively influence the research. Once the transcriptions were completed, all the interviews were personally translated into English.

The qualitative research analysis tool, NVivo 12, was used to analyze the data. Because "extensive interview texts" were analyzed, the data could be coded and condensed in order to "provide structure and give overviews."[15] Used was "coding": "attaching one or more keywords to a text segment in order to permit later identification of a statement."[16] The interview transcripts were uploaded into NVivo. Then research questions and interview questions were consulted to determine what the major themes were that needed to be coded by NVivo. Other major themes coded in NVivo were major themes not highlighted in my research questions or Interview Questions, but that were noticed as being relevant after interviewing all the interviewees and learning what themes were regularly emphasized and repeated within the interviewees as a whole. By using NVivo and a coding system, I was able to see the amount of relevant responses within each node. This helped me to understand the relevance of certain themes when I saw how many or how few people talked about that theme.

Each of the interview texts was read through on NVivo, and key words or phrases were searched. The entire interview was coded. For example, one key theme of the interviews was "finances." When the interviews were read through, parts were highlighted about "finances." Then the highlighted section was clicked and dragged into the node within the NVivo file that was related to "finances." Most of these codes followed the pattern of the seven interview questions. Then within each interview question the coding was separated into smaller nodes to separate each interview question into other smaller categories within the NVivo coding (e.g. first largest category "Factors in Retention," then smaller category "Most Important Factors for Retention," then smallest category "Family Support").

"Concept-driven coding" was primarily utilized, as previously developed concepts were used in the analysis.[17] Previously researched concepts from the literature review (e.g. pre-field training, finances, effectively building cross-cultural relationships) were consulted in order

---

15. Kvale and Brinkmann, *Interviews*, 201.
16. Kvale and Brinkmann, *Interviews*, 201–2.
17. Kvale and Brinkmann, *Interviews*, 202.

to determine the key themes that would be used in the NVivo coding. During the interviews, I was dependent on the perceptions of the informants, as they experienced their reality. I took these perceptions at face value, and tried to not second-guess or impose a foreign external meaning structure onto what they were saying.

Key quotes and general drifts and commonalities were searched. For example, a commonality that many of the interviewees had was talking about support of their families back in China as a pertinent factor in their remaining on the field. Family back home was also negatively significant, such as the challenges of when their family was unsupportive of them, or of not being allowed to fly home to see their family every year during Chinese New Year. In light of this, a separate node in the coding about family was created, although initially impact of the family was not expected to be a major theme.

Validity, Reliability, Possible Biases, and Permissions

Validity is defined as "the accuracy and trustworthiness of instruments, data, and findings in research."[18] Validity was increased by having clearly defined operational definitions, and adhering to those definitions the entire research process.[19] NVivo served to aid validation. Using computer software such as NVivo to analyze the data was beneficial in processing the data and identifying various themes. The interview questions were stated so that the interviewees could respond in ways that aided this investigation. A limited and purposive sample of Chinese missionaries was interviewed. Although the findings are not generalizable to all Chinese missionaries, underlying factors relevant to the experience of Chinese missionaries were discovered. The interviews were transcribed verbatim allowing the research subjects to describe their experiences in their own terms. Using only simple language in the interview questions and avoiding using technical jargon increased the validity of the research. Another component increasing validity was having an expert panel in the form of my doctoral committee. Another indication of the validity of the data is that most of the subjects spoke openly about struggles they had. So if they were trying to present a positive picture, they probably would not have been as open about some of the very personal struggles that they were facing. Their level of transparency,

---

18. Bernard, *Research Methods in Anthropology*, 53.
19. Bernard, *Research Methods in Anthropology*, 41.

especially coming from a shame-oriented culture and conversing with a total stranger, was surprising.

As an American who has lived for ten years in China, I realize I could be approaching this issue in a way that reflects certain Western values or expectations. By using a narrative interview approach, extra effort was given to let the interviewees express their own opinions. I aimed to not impose my American idea of what a good missionary is. As a stranger to these Chinese missionaries, they may have felt relaxed to honestly share their experiences. On the other hand, because I am a non-native Chinese speaker, and they did not know me, they may have felt reluctant to self-disclose. Ideally, their contact that introduced them to me could help quell any distrust or concerns.

Regarding permissions for the interviews, beforehand the Human Rights Protocol was approved by Trinity International University. Ethical considerations in this research were mentioned in the *Informed Consent Letter* (Appendix 2), which was translated into Chinese. This consent letter was emailed to the interviewees when we began our interview, so they could read through it while I read it to them. Then they verbally confirmed their consent to the interview. Before sending them the translated *Informed Consent Letter*, the first email correspondence (Appendix 3) with them identified who I am, how I obtained their contact information, and how I am doing research of Chinese missionaries and their adjustments in foreign cultures. They were asked if they could do an interview with me on WhatsApp or Skype that would last about 60 minutes, and they were reassured that the interview will remain confidential. I ensured they met interview requirements for my interview sample. I did not use transcribers or translators for the research, as the interviews were personally transcribed and translated.

4

Presentation of Findings

THIS CHAPTER PRESENTS THE findings from the interviews. The sections in this chapter represent each of the seven interview questions in the study. These are the interviewees': cross-cultural adjustment and coping on the field; experiences in pre-field training; cross-cultural relationships with hosts on the field; aptitude in learning the host language; experiences on the field when they have felt comfortable or uncomfortable; what factors have kept them on the field; and, other positive or negative experiences they have had. In each of the seven parts is a presentation of the findings, and a conclusion. After completing twenty interviews data saturation was reached, whereby responses were no longer yielding new information or insights.

The background information of the interviewees includes: their pseudonym; their marital status and if they have children; the region they are serving in on the mission field; how many years they have been serving in that country; their highest level of formal education; if their mission agency is international or a Chinese mission agency; their visa type; and, if they belong to a team.

The interviewees' pseudonym was established by first using "M" for male interviewees and "F" for female interviewees. Then the first number denotes how many years they have been on the mission field. The final number is an arbitrary number (1, 2, 3, etc.) that designates what number male "M" or female "F" they are on the list. For example, "M-10-8" represents a male "M" who has been on the field ten years "10," and is the eighth "8" male listed on this list. One point of clarity is that M-4-13 and F-4-9 are married and were interviewed together. This is why the below list has 26 names, rather than 25. For all other uses in this dissertation relating to the number of people interviewed 25 is used, and M-4-13 and F-4-9 are counted as one. This is the only case when this occurred in my research.

Table 4.1 Interviewees' Background Information

Pseudonym	Single/Married	Region Serving	Years Serving	Education Level	Mission Agency	Visa Type	Part of Team?
F-4-1	Single	Central Asia	4	undergrad	International	Student	Yes
F-5-2	Single	Middle East	5	undergrad	International	Tourist	Yes
F-5-3	Married	Central Asia	5	undergrad	International	Student	Yes
M-2.5-1	Married/Child	Middle East	2.5	middle school	Chinese	Tourist	Yes
M-2-2	Married/Child	Southeast Asia	2	middle school	Chinese	Volunteer	Yes
F-6-4	Married/Child	Central Asia	6	undergrad	Chinese	Work	Yes
F-3-5	Single	Middle East	3	undergrad	International	Tourist	Yes
M-3-3	Single	Southeast Asia	3	undergrad	Chinese	Work	Yes
M-3-4	Married/Child	Southeast Asia	3	undergrad	Chinese	Volunteer	Yes
M-8-5	Married/Child	Central Asia	8	master's	house church	Student	No
M-3-6	Married	Middle East	3	middle school	house church	Student	No
M-4-7	Married/Child	Central Asia	4	undergrad	International	Student	Yes
F-6-6	Single	Southeast Asia	6	Associate's	International	Work	Yes
M-10-8	Married/Child	Southeast Asia	10	middle school	Chinese	Work	Yes

PRESENTATION OF FINDINGS

Pseudonym	Single/ Married	Region Serving	Years Serving	Education Level	Mission Agency	Visa Type	Part of Team?
F-13-7	Single	Southeast Asia	13	MDiv	International	Work	Yes
M-5-9	Single	Southeast Asia	5	high school	International	Work	No
M-9-10	Married/ Child	Southeast Asia	9	middle school	Chinese	Social	No
M-8-11	Married/ Child	Southeast Asia	8	middle school	International	Work	Yes
F-3.5-8	Single	Central Asia	3.5	undergrad	International	Student	Yes
M-12-12	Married/ Child	Central Asia	12	middle school	Chinese	Work	Yes
M-4-13	Married/ Child	Southeast Asia	4	high school	Chinese	Work	Yes
F-4-9	Married/ Child	Southeast Asia	4	middle school	Chinese	Work	Yes
M-5-14	Married/ Child	Southeast Asia	5	high school	Chinese	Work	Yes
F-8-10	Single	Central Asia	8	undergrad	International	Work	Yes
F-7-11	Single	Southeast Asia	7	undergrad	International	Volunteer	Yes
M-5-15	Married/ Child	Southeast Asia	5	middle school	Chinese	Work	Yes

Summarizing the above background information, fifteen of the 25 interviewees were male and ten were female. Ten of the above were single: eight single women and two single men. Fifteen were married. All of these married had at least one child, except two married interviewees who did not have children. Of those thirteen who have children, nine of them have children of school age. Four of these parents have children who go to host schools in the host language. The other five interviewees with school age children have children who go to international schools taught in English. Of those who had children while on the field, some of the Chinese wives returned to China to have the child while the husband stayed on the field, with the husband and wife being separated from one another for multiple months. Others left the mission field together as a family and returned to China to have their child. Some had their children on the mission field without returning to China.

As far as regions in which the missionaries are serving, twelve of the 25 are in Southeast Asia; eight are in Central Asia; four are in the Middle East; and, one is in South Asia. Pertaining to their years on the field, ten of the 25 have been on the field between two to four years. Eleven have been on the field five to eight years. Four have been on the field nine or more years. Regarding what region of China is their hometown, eight of the 25 are from Eastern China and eight are from Central China. Three are from Northeast China and there are two from each of these regions: Southeast China, Northwest China, and Southwest China.

As for their educational background, thirteen of the 25 have at least a bachelor's degree, with two of the interviewees obtaining their bachelor's on the mission field. Eight missionaries' highest education is middle school. The highest education for three of them is high school. One of them has an associate's degree. Two of the interviewees have a master's degree, with one of them receiving an MDiv in the U.S. and one of them obtaining a bachelor's and master's on the field.

23 of the 25 interviewees are Han Chinese. M-9-10 is from the Li Su minority group. F-13-7 is half Man and half Han. Regarding the mission agency they were sent through, twelve of the 25 belong to international mission agencies. Eleven were sent through Chinese mission agencies. Two of the interviewees do not belong to mission agencies and were sent independently through house churches in China.

Relating to their form of visa on the field twelve of the 25 interviewees have work visas. Four of these teach Chinese; three run businesses; two have work visas but do not do business or work; one on the surface has a company, but does not do any work for the company; and, one has a missionary visa. Six of the 25 interviewees have a student visa. Four have volunteer visas. Three have tourist visas.

On the topic of their interaction with other missionaries, 21 of the 25 interviewees responded as belonging to a team. Those belonging to international mission agencies were more likely to have teams mixed with Chinese missionaries and missionaries from other countries. Some missionaries with Chinese agencies also belonged to teams of mixed nationalities. Other missionaries were on teams with host believers, including some interviewees belonging to international agencies and some with Chinese agencies. Some from Chinese agencies belonged to teams that were all Chinese, and they only interacted with Chinese missionaries. Others belonged to Chinese teams but also interacted with other missionaries from other countries. Three of the 25 interviewees lack any interaction with other Chinese. M-5-9 and M-5-14 are without having other Chinese missionaries near them. M-8-5 is unwilling to interact with Chinese missionaries, because of the tense security situation in China. Six of the 25 interviewees attend only a host church, which consists of those that: belong to a host team; minister with a host church; are planting a host church; or, others who attend only a host church.

The first research question addressed how Chinese cross-cultural workers have succeeded or struggled in cross-cultural relationships. It examined the prevailing impression of Chinese cross-cultural workers having difficulty in cross-cultural communication. Also of relevance for the study was analyzing how these Chinese cross-cultural workers adapted in learning the host language and assimilating to the host culture. Finally, the research investigated perceived factors that contributed to the more thriving Chinese cross-cultural workers developing effective cross-cultural relationships on the mission field.

The second research question in this research analyzed what pre-field and on the field experiences have contributed to Chinese cross-cultural workers' retention in cross-cultural service. This encompassed what pre-field preparation or on the field support has been useful to Chinese missionaries, and what kinds of pre-field preparation or on the field support they wish they had received, but did not. Support structures were analyzed, such as their home church support, teammates' support, mission agency, and other specific factors that have contributed to the missionaries' retention.

Cross-Cultural Adjustment and Coping

Easier Cross-Cultural Adjustments

For six of the interviewees, they experienced an easier move to the new country. Some of these were because their hometowns in China were similar to the environment, culture, and customs of the new country. F-6-4 said, "Because I am from far Northwest China, it was easier to adjust [to life in Central Asia]. The feeling of crossing cultures is not that obvious. My home is similar to here. When I moved here, I felt like I was still back in my home." F-8-10, who was from the same province in Northwest China, explained similarly how her culture shock living in Central Asia has been minimal.

M-8-11 expressed how his adjustment to Southeast Asia was smoother partly because he was from a similar place in Southwest China. He said, "The challenges were not enormous. My hometown is in Southwest China, so food and other aspects here are easier for me to accept."

M-5-9 explained how, because he grew up in a village in China, it was easier for him to serve as a missionary in a village in Southeast Asia. "My personal background is living in a village. I have not had too many problems living in a village on the field. I have adjusted well, whether that be with the poverty or with the host food."

An interviewee M-2-2 mentioned how living three years in another country before moving to his country helped his adjustment on the mission field. Two interviewees expressed how visiting that country short-term before they moved eased the adjustment there. F-8-10 said, "[I] came to this country twice before, so before [I] moved here [I] already was prepared. [I] knew what it was like here. This helped [me] have realistic expectations." M-8-11 similarly said, "For the two years before we moved here, I came here once a year and stayed for a month. This place was not unfamiliar for me."

Most Common Cross-Cultural Adjustment Challenges

The interviewees were asked what their largest cross-cultural adjustment challenges were during their first couple of years on the field. The most frequent response to this question (11 people) was with the food or drink in the new culture. Some interviewees expressed how they offended hosts because they refused to follow their eating habits. M-2-2 said, "In that country, they do not use chopsticks. We were in the mountains, and they used their hands to eat. For Chinese, we do not like to use our hands to eat. I went out to look for bamboo to make chopsticks, but when I was chopping the chopsticks, I cut my wrist with a knife. I had to go out of the way to find bamboo and try to make chopsticks. This showed the hosts that I had failed to accept them." Another interviewee M-5-9 similarly said, "In villages here, they will eat frogs, snakes, and spiders. I am afraid of snakes. One time the teacher went to the market and bought snakes, and came back to cook them for us. When I went to the kitchen and saw all those snakes, I refused to eat them. I left to go fishing because I did not want to eat what they were eating, as the other students were eating the snakes. My rejecting reactions and actions at that time must have offended the hosts."

Other interviewees had difficulties with adjusting to the host food initially, but eventually adapted. M-8-11 expressed, "For breakfast, they eat dried rice. For lunch, they eat dried rice. And for dinner, they have dried rice. When I came here I had to adapt to the food. Within a few months, I was able to adjust." Another interviewee M-3-6 had difficulty adjusting to the coffee culture in the Middle East. He said, "Drinking coffee [is a challenge]. People here drink bitter Arabic coffee all the time. Every time you meet you need to sit and have a cup of coffee. Now we are mostly used to this."

A common initial challenge for interviewees in cross-cultural adjustment was the language (10 people). Some interviewees felt like they were powerless to do anything themselves. F-3-5 said, "When I went out I could not understand anything. I always needed a translator. I felt like I could not do anything by myself."

Another challenge with the language was that they were unable to communicate with others to do outreach. M-3-4 said, "When we first got here the challenge of failing to know the language was huge. We could not communicate with others. I went to a university to meet students, but at that time we could not speak the host language. We tried to speak English with the students, but sometimes their English was poor."

Other interviewees expressed disappointment with their lack of language ability improvement after one or two years on the field. M-4-13 said, "I went to language class each day, but after my first year of language learning, I realized that my language ability was limited. I was unable to remember vocabulary words. I was so disappointed. I went shopping but had linguistic difficulties because of the tones. I did not know how to say what I desired to say. People often failed to understand what I was saying." Similarly, F-6-6 said, "I was working and studying language at the same time on my own because I had a full-time job. I progressed slower than others because I studied language off and on. This was stressful at first." F-4-9 explained her unique situation as a wife and mother, and said, "When we first moved here, we had a small baby I had to take care of at home, and I was unable to regularly go out and be with people. After a year here, my language was still terrible, which was stressful."

A common challenge in cross-cultural adjustment for the interviewees was with interpersonal relationships with hosts (9 people). Some interviewees said how they were uncomfortable with the hosts' relationship expectations. F-3-5 said, "The people here are easy to befriend. I can feel close to people even after we just met. My friends here want me to share everything with them about my life, which is hard for me. I feel like I need boundaries. This sometimes causes me stress."

Other interviewees expressed frustrations in misinterpreting what hosts were thinking. F-13-7 said, "When I have a conflict with a host person, I think they should understand what I am saying, but later I realize they failed to understand me. Sometimes I think I should understand what they are saying or how they perceive things, but later I realize that I did not grasp their thoughts at all."

F-3.5-8 had her money stolen from her by someone she considered to be her "best host friend." She said, "I had a host Muslim friend and thought we were great friends. She often came to our apartment. My roommate and I started to lose money. Later we found out that it was this Muslim friend who had been stealing money from our home. I thought I could trust her and that she trusted me. However, she ultimately stole our money." To resolve this problem, F-3.5-8 and her roommate confronted the Muslim friend. They told her how her stealing the money was contrary to the Bible's teachings. From this experience, F-3.5-8 learned that she must have more wisdom in interacting with host people because some host people are similar to her Muslim friend and would try to steal money from her. F-3.5-8 learned to better understand hosts' motives to be friends with her, whether it is because they are genuinely interested in the Christian faith, or because they think she is a wealthy foreigner and thus just want her money. At first, F-3.5-8 felt very angry and like she had been cheated. Nevertheless, she still never considered permanently leaving the country and moving back to China. But she realized that this negative experience was part of the host culture. This experience helped her better understand the hosts, as well as how poor they are and how much they may need money.

PRESENTATION OF FINDINGS

F-3-5 expressed frustration in having only shallow relationships with hosts. She said, "In my first year I often had trouble communicating deeply with others because of my language ability deficiencies. I made new friends but could only talk about shallow topics with them and have a surface level relationship with them."

Another challenge in living cross-culturally has been related to the host ways of life (7 people). A few interviewees were frustrated because of housing challenges. M-3-6 said, "When we first got here, our water was quickly all used up, and we did not know why. Our neighbors told us we had used all our water already. We failed to realize that we only received one small bucket of water per week to use." M-4-13 disapproved of how the hosts disposed of their trash. He said, "They put the trash out for a long time then burned the trash. It was so putrid. So I started weekly throwing our trash away at a friend's home, which offended host people. They thought I was disapproving how they took care of trash and looking down on them." M-4-13 was surprised that the hosts were offended by his actions, as throwing away trash seemed like such a common activity to do. From this experience, M-4-13 learned that he needed to use host methods to dispose of the trash, rather than his own methods. Otherwise, the hosts would be offended. He learned that the next time a similar situation occurs he, before making a decision, needs to be careful and ask the hosts how they would deal with it. An interviewee had difficulties with the host religious practices. M-5-15 said, "A challenge is that it is a Buddhist country. If they are on the road or anywhere where they see idols, they will stop and worship the idol." F-8-10 had struggles with the host customs in Central Asia of regularly kissing each other. She said, "When people see each other, they will kiss each other's face two or three times. At first, I hated this."

A prevalent challenge in cross-cultural adjustment was with hosts' perceptions of time (6 people). Some have been infuriated by this. F-7-11 said, "In China, people will not arrive too late. However, hosts are particularly unpunctual. When I first arrived, I set a time to meet host friends. We said to meet at 3 pm, but when I went at 3 pm I failed to see them. I waited until 4 or 4:30 pm till they came. After two or three or five times [of this happening], I was furious."

Six interviewees expressed challenges with team conflict. Some had challenges in joining an international team. M-3-4 said, "People from many countries were on our team. We had to adapt to having multiple cultures within our team. This was a challenge. We had different ideas.

Coming from a monocultural context like China, and entering a multicultural team in Southeast Asia, it was hard. My wife was stressed during that time." Similarly, F-6-6 said, "We had team problems. I am the only one from China. Teammates were from Taiwan, Hong Kong or Singapore, and could speak Chinese. Nevertheless, trying to minister together we had different types of conflict. We had different ways to do things. Interpersonal relationships were hard for me."

Other interviewees had conflicts with Chinese teammates. F-5-3 expressed, "I had a Chinese roommate who was my teammate. When we lived together I realized our personalities are incompatible for living together. I felt exhausted living with her."

F-3-5 noted challenges in adjusting to an international church. She said, "A challenge in my first year was going to an international church. Everything was in English. I was not used to listening to sermons in English. Because everything was in English I felt like I failed to be encouraged spiritually during the weekly Sunday time at church."

Four people had challenges related to ministry. M-3-3 said, "My first year here the chief stress was working in the orphanage. That was my first time to be with so many children. These children could only speak the host language, but at that time I was unable to speak it. Additionally, we were stressed because we had insufficient workers at the orphanage."

Three interviewees mentioned challenges with their visa. M-2-2 said, "We have to travel within China each time we need to take care of our visa. Large amounts of our energy, time and money have gone into taking care of our visa. One-third of our financial support each year from China is used for taking care of our visa. This is our most significant stress." M-5-14 had similar challenges in South Asia, saying, "The main challenge has been my wife and child's inability to obtain a long-term visa. We have about six months apart every year. Each time my family comes they can only stay for three months. Then they have to go back to China. Then they need to stay in China at least two months before they can apply for another visa. It is awful! It is hard for Chinese to come to this country in South Asia because this country and China have a bad relationship." M-2.5-1 commented on the stresses of his visa. He said, "We want to stay here long-term. We need a job that gives us a visa, but visa issues are a headache. It is hard to find a job. It is hard for foreigners to run a business in the Middle East. What can we do so that we can stay long-term? Before we had a three-month tourist visa and had to leave the country every three months to renew it. This is feasible but stressful. I can do this, but not long-term."

A challenge for three interviewees was adjusting to the weather, especially in a hotter climate. M-5-15 said, "The hardest aspect in Southeast Asia is the weather, where every day is about 34 or 35 degrees Celsius, or even over 40 degrees. I am from Northeast China, from a cold place. When I first came here, this was a huge challenge for me."

Two single women on the mission field expressed disgust in how the host men treat them. F-3-5 said, "The principal challenge in the Middle East has been with the host men. I will often be walking on the road and a group of men will yell to me and say 'Are you married?' or 'How old are you?' This always makes me feel uncomfortable." F-3-5 said how she had not been physically threatened or abused by host men. She did discuss these problems with her mission agency leaders. She resolved tensions with host men by praying about these challenges and having a meeting with her leaders to discuss this dynamic. As a result, F-3-5 ministers only among host women, and not host men. If she sees host men, she will only have a basic conversation with them. In addition, single woman F-4-1 expressed her fear of going outside late at night by herself because she felt unsafe.

Two interviewees' main challenges in adjustment have been with their families. F-6-4 said, "For our family, in our first year here we met challenges with sicknesses. The medical care is poor and some medical terms I cannot understand in Russian. We did not know what to do when we had health problems." M-2.5-1 said, "Conflict exists between me and my wife. In cross-cultural situations with great stress, sometimes it is impossible to talk to my wife. We have problems at home. This stress causes problems between my wife and me."

Two of the interviewees struggled with intense loneliness. M-3-4 said, "An early challenge was loneliness. We were void of any friends. We were the only family here from China. We could not communicate with others. Sometimes when we were unable to talk to others, we felt homesick and lonely. That stress was large at that time." M-3-6 talked about the culture shock and loneliness he experienced, and how he did not even want to go outside or meet people. M-3-6 said, "When I had been in the Middle East around three months, I experienced intense culture shock because of multiple factors, and did not even want to go outside. I did not want to see anyone or make new friends. When we went out, host children would say many dirty words. When we went out we were afraid that the children were going to grab rocks and hit us with them. We did not even want to leave our home."

Coping with Cross-Cultural Challenges

The interviewees had different ways to cope with their cross-cultural adjustment difficulties. In coping with homesickness, some of the interviewees talked to family and friends in China on video. F-4-1 said, "In that first year, during the Spring Festival [nine years ago], I was terribly homesick, and I had technical challenges talking to my family. Now I can talk to them using a video whenever I want, so I struggle less with homesickness."

M-3-6 expressed how another method to cope with homesickness was to learn the language and make host friends. He said, "We were homesick our first year here, but I slowly adjusted to the life here. I started learning the language and visiting host friends."

Two mentioned how moving to the mission field with a large group of Chinese missionaries ameliorated homesickness and culture shock. M-10-8 said, "More than ten of us moved here together. We did not miss home as much, because all of us were Chinese who knew each other well. We felt like a family. At first, we were homesick but slowly it became less intense." M-12-12 similarly said, "When we first moved here, we were a part of a team of ten or fifteen Chinese people who moved together and lived together. This helped eradicate some culture shock when we arrived." M-12-12 described how one reason the mission agency sent so many people together was to reduce loneliness and culture shock for the missionaries. A problem, however, was that he and his teammates were always together, so they had very little interaction with hosts or the host culture. So it was difficult to trust the hosts, and for a while, they had no close host friends.

Two others noted how they were accustomed to living far away from their hometowns, so they did not feel overly homesick on the mission field. M-5-14 said, "Beginning in 2007, I have adapted to being away from my family. I do not call them often. Before I moved to South Asia, I was already used to seeing my family very little."

F-6-4 stressed how a contributor for alleviating her homesickness was her mother and home church's support for her. She said, "My mother is a believer. We have a house church in my home in Northwest China. Though I may feel homesick, I know they are praying for me, which helps me feel better."

As far as coping with the cross-cultural challenge of the food, five people failed to adapt to the host food, so they stopped eating out. M-8-5 said, "Food is less diverse than in China which has many choices. We rarely eat out and cook more at home."

Other interviewees coped with adjustment difficulties by clarifying their calling and adapting to the cultures. M-9-10 said, "In coping with the challenge of dirty markets and buying food that was not fresh, we needed to clarify our calling. If I can clarify my calling, I can know that God called me here, and I will realize my difficulties [with host food] are not that significant." Similarly, M-10-8 said, "I changed myself to adjust to the host culture, weather, and method of doing things."

In regards to challenges with hosts' perception of time, some interviewees, though meeting initial difficulties, have eventually adapted to the hosts' time perceptions. M-12-12 said, "Though initially, it was hard to adjust to the hosts' time perceptions, now in some ways I am slower than the hosts. Sometimes host friends will criticize me for being late. I tell them 'Yes. I am a host. I look like a Chinese person, but actually, I am a host.'" M-4-7 said, "Before I go out I first call people to remind them we are meeting, to ensure they have already left their home. When I am waiting for him I can have a book to read." F-3.5-8 has adapted to the host time culture by calling them several times in advance as a reminder. She said, "When setting up a meeting with friends here a week in advance, the day before we are to meet I need to remind them we are meeting the same day. Then she can remember."

M-8-5 explained how learning their language and culture helped with adjusting to difficulties with their time perceptions. He said, "The first year when they arrived late it would infuriate me. Learning their culture, background, and language helped me cope with this. In doing this, I could adjust to their culture."

For resolving team conflict, M-3-4 said it requires dialoguing and becoming familiar with one another. He said, "To persevere through challenges [with international team conflict], my wife and I found time to drink coffee together with them and chat. This was how we dealt with it: talking many times with each other, one on one and face-to-face. It took a while and regularly talking together to resolve these issues with one another."

Another interviewee noted how a mentor helped them resolve their team conflict. F-7-11 said, "A mentor from the agency helped us with team conflict. The mentor gave us direction and helped us resolve issues in our relationship and to think using a different perspective. By doing this, I could have reconciliation with my co-worker."

In coping with intense loneliness in the Middle East and not wanting to leave his home, M-3-6 talked about how he started painting. He said, "Before I seldom painted, but during that hard time, I bought paintbrushes and painted at home. This helped me persevere through our hardest time here." Another technique to cope with loneliness was with M-3-4, who mentioned how it was valuable for him and his wife to endure through the loneliness they felt on the mission field by talking to family and friends in China.

In facing the challenge of language learning, interviewees noted how starting to learn the language aided them in overcoming their initial challenges with the language. M-8-11 said, "The prime challenge was being unable to speak the language. This caused great stress for our lives. I had a Chinese missionary friend who could guide me. I started learning the language and learned with him, and my language slowly improved." M-5-15 said, "My first few years here I was unable to learn the language, so I could not pronounce their sounds; however, God led me to begin a language program last year. Now I can gradually speak more. I have overcome this language obstacle."

In regards to coping with interpersonal challenges in adjusting, F-5-2 was helped by learning the language and taking teammates with her to meet hosts. She said, "I improved my language, adjusted to life here, and was less tired than before to be with hosts. I had the energy to be with them. Also beneficial was inviting one of my teammates to go with me to meet host friends. This made it more relaxed."

M-10-8 thought a key in improving interpersonal relationships with hosts was to change the hosts' misconceptions. He said, "When we came here, hosts asked us, 'You are Chinese but you are poor. What are you doing here?' To overcome this, we could slowly change their misconceptions. They could get to know us well. This process was difficult because some people did not want to be friends with us."

In adapting to the host culture, two men said they adapted to not using paper while using the bathroom. M-5-14 said, "People in South Asia do not use paper when using the bathroom, and use their hands to eat. I slowly adjusted to doing this."

F-5-3 noted how it is advantageous to study the host culture so as to adjust in the new culture. She said, "I thought I needed to study and take initiative to try to see similarities between hosts and Chinese. So I did research and my first year I went to a seminar. I found resources online to understand their culture and history. This was helpful for me."

In adapting to having different transportation on the mission field, M-2-2 said, "In this country, they drive fast. There are few traffic lights. They drive on the left side. When I came to this place I realized I needed to drive like them so I would not crash. I had to adjust."

To avoid being cheated by host drivers in Southeast Asia, F-13-7 said, "[After being cheated badly by a taxi driver] I learned from others names of bridges and roads. Then when I took a taxi, I could clearly tell the driver the directions to get there. He would be afraid to take the wrong route. I spent about a year learning all this, to solve these problems."

Concluding the cross-cultural adjustment and adaption section, several of the interviewees had easier adjustments in moving to the mission field. Those who grew up in environments similar to where they were moving on the mission field had a smoother adjustment. Chinese missionaries experienced numerous challenges in adjusting to life in the new context. Some of the most prevalent challenges were related to the food, language, interpersonal relationships with hosts, hosts' perception of time, and team conflict. The Chinese missionaries had various ways to cope with these difficulties.

Pre-Field Preparation

Of the 25 interviewees, eleven had three to six months of total pre-field missionary preparation of some kind. Two had seven to eleven months; three had one to two years; and, nine had over two years. For some of these, part of this preparation would be English language acquisition. For others it may be taking short-term mission trips to reach minority groups in China. Or it could be other forms of "mission training" or attending a seminary for theological education.

Table 4.2 Interviewees' Missionary Preparation

Pseudo-nym	Mission Training	Theological Education	Also Included
F-4-1	3 months	none	
F-5-2	3 months	none	
F-5-3	3 months	none	
M-2.5-1	1 year	none	short-term missions
M-2-2	1 year	2 years	short-term missions
F-6-4	2 years	none	short-term missions
F-3-5	3 months	none	
M-3-3	8 months	2 years	English learning
M-3-4	3 months	2 years	short-term missions
M-8-5	none	8 months	English learning
M-3-6	2.5 years	none	vocational training, English learning
M-4-7	3 months	none	
F-6-6	3 months	none	short-term missions
M-10-8	6 months	none	English learning
F-13-7	1 year	3 years	
M-5-9	3 months	none	
M-9-10	1 year	3 years	short-term missions
M-8-11	1 year	1 year	short-term missions
F-3.5-8	3 months	none	
M-12-12	1 year	1 year	vocational training
M-4-13	3 months	none	short-term missions
F-4-9	3 months	none	short-term missions
M-5-14	2 years	1 year	short-term missions, English learning
F-8-10	3 months	none	
F-7-11	1 year	none	short-term missions
M-5-15	8 months	none	English learning

Of the 25 interviewees, 24 received mission training. Only M-8-5 failed to receive any mission training. Of those who received mission training, one had under three months. Eleven had three to six months; three had seven to eleven months; five had one to two years; two had at least two years; and, two had combined theological and mission training for over two years. Most of those who received three months total of mission training belonged to international mission agencies. Those who belonged to international mission agencies that had three-month training studied these subjects: cultural differences in that country; managing culture shock; language learning methods; adapting on the field; team dynamics; one's personal relationship with God; how God views missions; how to live on the field if one is single or married; stress management; and, better knowing the gospel. Others within their mission training in addition to the subjects listed above also studied mission history, or had classes focused on Muslim or other specific outreach.

For most of the interviewees who had overall missionary preparation for at least a year, short-term mission trips were a component of their preparation. These trips consisted of ministering for days or for months among minority groups inside or outside China.

Analyzing theological education for the 25 interviewees, twelve had theological education. Thirteen of the interviewees lacked having any theological education. Two had three months or less; two had four to eight months; two had one year; three had at least two years; and, two had combined theological and mission training for over two years. The theological education mentioned by the interviewees included learning subjects such as these in an underground and informal seminary in China: preaching; pastoring; counseling; Systematic Theology; and, studying all the books of the Bible.

Most Helpful Pre-field Preparation They Received

Many interviewees (6 people) noted the importance of theological education they received. Some said it gave them a strong theological foundation. M-3-4 said, "The two years at the Bible school in China were helpful for me. I could understand and be familiar with the whole Bible, all 66 books, which I read numerous times. We memorized Scriptures. I could have a strong biblical foundation. This is valuable now because it has aided me in becoming someone who has a daily habit to read and understand the Bible." M-9-10 said, "The most helpful before I came on the field was studying Systematic Theology, which facilitated me having a biblical foundation of the truth and better grasping the gospel." Another interviewee M-3-3 expressed how he would not still be on the mission field if not for his theological foundation. He said, "If I was without my theological foundation, it would be hard to persevere here for so long because living in a foreign land is stressful." F-13-7 thought that her theological education was helpful for her because she could shepherd herself. She said, "This theological education caused my entire doctrinal framework to be clear. My theological education gives me the ability to shepherd myself when I feel lonely or meet other problems. My seminary life has been the main force and motivator for me."

Many of the interviewees went on pre-field short-term mission trips. Most of these short-term mission trips were multiple months or a year in length, ministering among minority groups in Western China or in other countries. Some of these interviewees (6 people) specifically expressed how these short-term mission trips were particularly helpful preparation for them going to the mission field. Some mentioned how these trips were advantageous so they could experience cross-cultural living. M-3-3 said, "During the year in that country, we could experience for ourselves cross-cultural living. When I moved to Southeast Asia, it was helpful I could have previous experience of cross-cultural living because of the year in that other country." M-2.5-1 noted how short-term mission trips were helpful to him because he could learn adaptability. He said, "I could live in host peoples' homes, eat their food, and learn their language. At first, I felt my culture was superior to theirs, but later I understood them, learned their culture and adapted to life there. This adaptability that I developed in that country was helpful for when I moved to the Middle East. I could respect their culture and try to use their approach to life to do things." M-4-13 expressed how short-term missions were profitable to him because it aided him in practically thinking about his surroundings and experiences. He said, "During the short-term missions, I was forced to practically think about my surroundings. We have used these skills for thinking about what we see and experience on the field."

Regarding those who mentioned topics related to personal spiritual disciplines, two commented on the helpfulness during missionary training of learning about developing one's spiritual life. M-5-9 said valuable to him was developing spiritual life practices. He said, "Important was developing a spiritual life. The teachers emphasized that once you move on the mission field, you will have many challenges with your spiritual life. You must learn how to feed yourself." For F-5-3's preparation, advantageous was emphasizing how God is most concerned about our personal condition rather than our accomplishments. She said, "They emphasized that God cares most about our personal condition, rather than about our accomplishments on the mission field." F-3.5-8 noted how learning how to rest was helpful for her. She said, "The most beneficial to me was the training about having rest time. Each week we need to set aside a half a day or a full day to rest and take a break from life."

As for language related benefits of training, three people mentioned how studying language learning methods was helpful for them in missionary preparation. F-6-6 said it gave her a pace for language learning. She said, "The teacher taught us skills and methods of language learning, which gave me a pace and helped me understand at what stage I am at in language study, and how to reach higher levels. When I studied the host language I could evaluate myself, to see where I was improving and where I needed to improve." M-3-3 thought helpful to him was English language acquisition. He said, "English is our language of communication. We could not speak the host language, so we needed English to communicate."

Pertaining to beneficial parts of training that were focused more specifically on ministry or missions, M-8-11 noted how receiving shepherding training was helpful for him. He said, "My training included pastoral training. I often shepherd host people. Everything I studied in the school has benefited my shepherding of hosts here." Profitable for M-2.5-1 was learning about mission needs. He said, "I could learn about the many places around the world and their mission needs, and how I could contribute in reaching those needs." M-5-14 was encouraged by reading biographies of missionaries. He said, "We received little booklets with missionary biographies on them. Reading these little booklets was beneficial for me. Missionary biographies have helped me in continuing to be on the mission field until now."

Some of the interviewees noted parts of their training that benefitted their adjustment on the field. Two interviewees said how it was valuable to be told by the trainers what difficulties they should expect to meet on the mission field. F-5-2 said, "Helpful in the training was that I could learn what stresses I would experience on the mission field. These kinds of stress are normal on the mission field. I could feel less stressed when life was difficult." Profitable to F-4-1 was learning about the cycle on the mission field. She said, "Studying the process of the cycle in missions helped me. When I had situations happening in my life, I knew which phase in the adjustment process I was in and that this is normal to experience. This aided me in mitigating my stress." A helpful component of F-8-10's training was the trainers telling her to find aspects on the mission field that she enjoyed. She said, "Learning how to enjoy life on the mission field was constructive. This included how to find host places where we like to eat, or coffee shops or Chinese restaurants. They taught us to have hobbies, like exercising or swimming."

Others mentioned other aspects of their preparation that were beneficial to them. M-12-12 said vocational training was beneficial for him. He said, "Vocational training was helpful because this helped us to have an authentic identity here." Helpful for F-6-4 in developing teamwork was to do everything together as a team during training. She said, "In China, we did our training together in a team, which was effective preparation for coming on the mission field, being a part of a team, and having everyone work together."

Table 4.3 Most Helpful Pre-Field Preparation They Received

Most Helpful Pre-field Preparation They Received	# of Respondents
Theological Education	6
Short-term Missions	6
Studying Language Learning Methods	3
Learning Challenges often Experienced on Field	2
Developing One's Spiritual Life	2

Pre-field Preparation They Wish They Had Received, but Had Not

The most prevalent (twelve of 25 respondents) pre-field preparation the interviewees wish they had received but did not was vocational training. Some noted how vocational training would help them find a job, earn money, and provide for themselves. M-8-5 said, "Most important is to receive vocational training, to be able to work within the community. I think I am lacking in this. Without these skills, it is hard to find a job here and earn money."

PRESENTATION OF FINDINGS

Similarly, M-2-2 added, "My missionary preparation lacked training on how to use business on the field for the purpose of missions. Financial support from China is insufficient and our expenses for our visa take up one-third of this money. So we are constantly trying to solve this problem: How can we provide for our family on our own through having a business?" M-3-3 said, "It would have been of benefit to receive vocational training before coming here, so we could have provided for ourselves and found a job quickly after we got here. We would not have to fear being without money if churches in China stopped supporting us. Through having a real job, we can through that job meet more host people than if we were without a job or skills here. Our preparation did not have [vocational training]."

On the topics of a lack of financial support and needing to work on the field, M-5-15 talked about how he had to work in a factory his first year on the field, because of receiving insufficient financial support from China. He said, "When I first moved here I thought I needed to work full-time in the factory. I worked in the factory for over a year, because at that time I did not have any support from a church."

As for the need for receiving vocational training, M-3-6 thought it would provide a platform and position in the society. He said, "I now have a student visa for a third year, but I cannot continue to have a student visa long-term if we want to stay long-term. Otherwise, others will be suspicious of us. They will think 'Where does your money come from?'" On the topic of obtaining a visa and having a legitimate status on the mission field, F-4-1 said, "We have to undertake our visa on our own. It would have been beneficial to have this preparation. I wish I had preparation and support in obtaining a legitimate visa and status here."

F-8-10 similarly noted how vocational training is necessary for serving on the field long-term. She said, "We cannot always use student visas. How to find and maintain a job on the mission field is more practical and critical preparation than theological education. I wish I had training on this."

M-5-9 expressed how skill training would be something he could pass on to host Christians. He said, "My burden is to minister to the villagers here, but pastors in villages are without salaries, and they need to support their family from farming. I want to learn skill training, and I want to take my skill and pass it on to the hosts."

F-3.5-8, who is a Chinese teacher, wishes that before she arrived on the field she could have received a Chinese teaching certification.

Another preparation that four interviewees wish they had received but did not was English language acquisition. Some expressed how their deficiency in English skills has made it impossible to communicate with other missionaries. M-2-2 said, "I cannot understand more complex English. When I communicate with other missionaries, I cannot understand many words they say. Sometimes when I work together with them, I feel like language is an obstacle." Others note how learning English would benefit them with ministry. M-8-11 said, "Studying English in China before coming would help me for when I first moved here. Young people here can speak English. However, when we moved here we were unable to speak English, and we could not speak the host language."

Three people wished they had received theological education, but they did not. Some mentioned how it would help them minister on the field. M-4-13 said, "I wish we had more theological education. In my four years here, sometimes people have asked me questions. When we share with others, I could be better equipped to share with them." M-4-7 said, "Something we have lacked is that we have been incapable of discussing with others deeper theological topics. One reason this would be valuable for me is that we are in a Muslim context, and often we have discussions with them about our faith. We need to understand how to converse about the Bible and Islam with these people." M-4-7 talked about how his previous training for ministry among Muslims was the Camel method[1] for evangelism among Muslims. He interacted mostly with highly educated Sunni Muslims. He would discuss with them the love of God, sin of man, and redemption and life of Jesus. He has read some of the Qur'an and some popular Christian books on Islam that had been translated into Chinese, such as *Jesus and Muhammad* and *Seeking Allah, Finding Jesus*. He said there are few books on ministry to Muslims that have been translated into Chinese, so his reading options in this area are limited.

Two people explained how it would have been helpful to have specific cultural training. F-3-5 said, "Of benefit would be if we had training that taught us about the particular culture that we were going to move into." M-3-6 said, "In our training in the Philippines, we did not meet many Muslims. When we moved here, Muslims were a new group within which to minister. This was a deficiency in our training."

---

1. The Camel method seeks to convert Muslims to Christianity by beginning with passages about Jesus in the Qu'ran.

F-5-2 thought it would have been beneficial to have international team training. She said, "I wish I had previous experience ministering together with people from other countries. In ministering for five years in China, I only ministered with other Chinese, but my team here is international. Our leader is Korean. It would have been useful before I left to minister together with people from other countries." F-6-6 and F-5-2 thought valuable would be to have conflict resolution training.

M-3-6 said it would have been helpful to take a short-term mission trip to the Middle East before they moved there. He said, "It would have been advantageous to come here for a short-term mission trip before moving here, so I would know beforehand about the difficulty in finding jobs here. I could have sufficiently prepared in China before moving here and learned beforehand how to start a business or find a job here."

M-10-8 noted lacking support raising training. He said, "A deficiency in the training was learning how to raise money. This is vital because for our ministry and our lives we need to raise support, and now we have inadequate funds."

In concluding this section on the interviewees' pre-field preparation, all of the interviewees received missionary preparation of at least three months. Approximately half of the interviewees received theological education, with seven interviewees having at least one year of full-time theological education. As for the question of the most helpful preparation they received, the most predominant responses were that theological education and short-term mission trips benefited them. In regards to the pre-field preparation they wish they had received but did not, twelve of the 25 people said they wished they had vocational training, which was undoubtedly the most widespread response to this question. Many of these respondents commented on how having vocational training would help them find a job, earn money, provide for themselves, meet new people, have a legitimate position in the society, and obtain a visa. Other than this response, four people wished they had received English language acquisition. Three people wished they had received theological education.

Table 4.4 Pre-Field Preparation They Wish They Had Received, but Did Not

Pre-field Preparation They Wish They Had Received, but Did Not	# of Respondents
Vocational Training	12
English Language Acquisition	4
Theological Education	3
Training of Culture they Would Minister In	2

Cross-Cultural Relationships

Factors in Making Closer Relationships

As for factors in making closer relationships with hosts, eight interviewees mentioned the relevance of helping hosts in various regards. M-12-12 emphasized the importance of not just helping his host friends, but also letting his host friends help him. He said, "For closer nonbelieving host friends, I will ask them to come and help me when one of our children is sick. We both have children. They are willing to come and help. In this way we are able to become friends: I need him, and he needs me." Other interviewees described making tight friendships by helping them. F-6-4 said, "I will talk to the wife and stay by her. When they do any housework, I will help them do it. They trust us. When we go back to China and then return here they are elated to see us. It is easy to be with them. They see us as one of their relatives." F-7-11 said, "It is imperative to serve them with a sincere heart and care for their needs. I can consider how I can help them in various practical ways, so they may know I respect them." M-5-9 said, "A host friend left to be a sailor in China. Before he left, he invited me to visit his home. I went to his home and met his family. When he left for China, I often went to their home to visit his family. This was touching for him. His mother told him, 'You have this kind of friend.'"

Seven interviewees mentioned the significance of having sufficient language ability for making close friends. F-8-10 said, "The first is language. If language is inadequate, this is a huge obstacle." F-5-2 said, "Having improved language ability makes it easier now to talk to them, and they can be relaxed." F-13-7 said, "It is necessary to speak the language fluently, to let hosts know that you respect their language."

Others expressed how language deficiencies can be an obstacle to making friends. F-6-6 said, "I still have barriers in my friendships with hosts, because of my language limitations. I want to become deeper friends with hosts, but language is an obstacle." Similarly, M-4-13 said, "I have wanted to make host friends, but after my first couple of years here I did not have any host friends. Sometimes I want to go talk to others but cannot clearly say to them what I desire to say." M-5-15 said, "We still do not express words clearly. The major obstacle to making friends is our language limitations."

Other interviewees have developed deeper relationships with host nonbelievers by visiting them and inviting them to their homes. F-6-4 said, "Sometimes we invite them to our homes to eat. Though they are devout Muslims, they know about our faith. We do not eat pork. They trust us and they come to our house to eat, and we go to their homes to eat." Others mention common meals as a way of building relationships. Similarly, three interviewees commented on how cooking for hosts aids in having closer relationships.

Three interviewees noted the importance of respecting hosts. M-4-13 said, "First is respecting them, and not looking down on them. This attitude is key. The person must think you respect them." M 5-9 said, "I respect them which is important. When I am with them, I am willing to become a listener."

Three noted how caring for the hosts builds tighter relationships. F-5-3 said, "Caring for other people is critical, and they can know that you care for them. When others are sick, I visit them. When I have nothing to do, I send them messages. When others need assistance, I help them with what they need to do."

Three interviewees have built closer relationships by being like the hosts. F-6-4 said, "I speak to them in their language and try to do things how they do them. I wear a head covering and a long dress to go to the Muslim village. When I am with them, they think I am one of them. Sometimes I cook together with them. They are farmers, so I go with them to the fields. This eases making friends." M-5-14 said, "Because I am easygoing, I will stay in their homes. They do not have beds and sleep on the floor. It is dirty, but I am willing to live with them. Our relationship is great. Being without electricity or Internet is not a problem for me. Hosts are likely to welcome and accept me because I am willing to live like them and with them."

Analyzing factors mentioned that are related to the interviewees' personality, two were helped in their relationships by their steady personality. F-6-6 said, "I am easy-going. When with me, they do not feel any pressure. They think I not only teach them Chinese, but I am like their older sister and can chat with them. I can have fun with them and spend time with them." Two noted an extroverted personality that benefits them. M-4-7 noted how his friendliness has helped him. He said, "When I go with others to see their host friends and their host friends see me they think I am friendly. They are willing to talk to me and open up to me the first time we meet. My friendliness helps people feel relaxed."

Pertaining to other factors for the interviewees making deeper relationships, M-12-12 mentioned how working with them facilitates in building relationships. M-3-6 described how his relationships became closer when they had fun together. F-7-11 talked about her taking the initiative helped her in building relationships. A factor for M-3-4 was that he is skilled at asking questions.

M-2.5-1 formed an intimate bond with his landlord. He said, "My son played with our landlord's children. We were good friends and often ate together. When they needed any assistance, I helped them. When they had a wedding in their family, I attended it together with my landlord. Or when they had parties or funerals, I went together with him. He saw me as one of their family members."

F-13-7 underscored the importance of not criticizing their culture. She said, "I have learned to appreciate beautiful aspects of their culture, rather than to criticize their culture. It is paramount to learn to respect, and even to go and learn about these cultural elements."

One interviewee expressed how being vulnerable to hosts led to the hosts openly sharing their struggles with her. F-7-11 said, "I stayed in a Muslim village for about three years. The first two years we played with the children, but others in the village did not even talk to us. The third year I started going to this village by myself once a week. By going by myself, I touched the hosts. When I started talking to many women, they were willing to share their struggles with me."

As for analyzing where the interviewees met their host friends, eight of them mentioned it was through teaching Chinese. Some teach Chinese in a language center. Other interviewees met their host friends through teaching them Chinese for free. Other interviewees commented on meeting other teachers through teaching Chinese. F-13-7 said, "My co-worker is a cute host woman. We eat together or go shopping. We are great friends, and we can trust one another. We have known each other thirteen years. We often take walks and eat together." Other interviewees who teach Chinese said they meet students from their classes and spend time together. Other interviewees met their closest host friends at a school where they were not employed. Two of the interviewees were full-time college students at the host college. Another interviewee F-5-2 met host friends while ministering at a host college where she did not work or study.

Three met host friends while playing sports. F-4-9 said about her husband M-4-13, "My husband likes to play basketball. He often plays at the college and I go with him. While he was playing, I met a girl student. I realized she and I had commonalities. The girl and I were always happy to talk. We have become good friends. When I have questions about anything, I ask her."

As far as other ways that interviewees met their host friends, six interviewees became close friends with a host teammate or roommate. Other interviewees mentioned difficulties in ministering with their host teammates. Five interviewees became friends with their neighbors. Five interviewees met their closest host friends in a host church. Two became friends with their language teacher. M-3-3 met host friends that were co-workers in the orphanage where he worked and ministered. M-3-6 met friends through tutoring children. M-4-7 met a host friend while sharing the gospel with people in a park.

Some interviewees had negative relationship experiences with hosts. M-12-12 explained, "I have a taxi driver near us. Every time we go out we will use his taxi, and the first time we bargained and he said we were 'friends'. I thought I would not have to bargain with him each time I used his taxi since we were 'friends', but I have been surprised that we have had to bargain. One time I did not ask the price when I got in his taxi, and he overcharged me significantly once I arrived."

What Interviewees Appreciate about Host Culture

Concerning what the interviewees appreciate about the host culture or people, five noted their politeness or friendliness. M-5-14 said, "South Asians are friendly so it is easy to build relationships with them. In the train, you can easily talk to a stranger."

Four interviewees commented on the hosts' passion and hospitality. M-10-8 said, "I like their hospitable attitude. When we go to their homes, they hospitably will take care of us. We will drink tea with them, and chat with them. Even if you are a stranger, they will still enthusiastically take care of you, and give you water to drink. Sometimes they will cook for you, even if they do not know you. They are willing to welcome others."

Three mentioned how they appreciate the hosts' simplicity. F-7-11 said, "I think they are simplistic. If you leave your key outside for a whole night, the key will still be in the door the next morning. You look for your key the next morning and cannot find it, and realize it is still hanging in the door outside. If this were to happen in China, your key would be gone long ago."

Three interviewees appreciate how the hosts respect their elders. F-8-10 said, "They are respectful of those older than them. As I get older, they respect me more, which I like." Others noted hosts' helpfulness. M-9-10 said, "I may not know them but I ask them for directions. They will immediately tell us the directions in a friendly manner."

F-5-2 likes how hosts express their emotions. She said, "People here more directly express their emotions. In China, people rarely say, 'I love you', but here they frequently do. They like to use body language in meeting others, which I like."

F-3-5 appreciates how Middle Easterners like to spend extensive time together. She said, "I like how they are willing to spend much time together, sitting with you at a place and chatting. This is their culture. They often go with their friends to coffee shops to drink coffee or tea."

M-4-7 likes how the hosts emphasize relationships. He said, "Relationships are important to them. Men have many friends. Sometimes when I meet someone, they help introduce me to all their other friends. They often talk and see each other. When I see my friend, he will always be together with his friends."

F-6-6 likes how hosts are accepting. She said, "Sometimes in China, I felt inferior to others and did not have self-confidence, but people here compliment others. Being in this environment helps me to be willing to open up myself to others. I feel confident. This causes me to want to be friends with them."

Aspects of Host Culture Dislike

As far as aspects about the host culture or people they dislike, eight interviewees mentioned what they perceive as dishonesty and corruption of the host culture and people. Some described the hosts telling lies. M-12-12 said, "Workers tell me they need to ask for a leave of absence and want an advance payment from me. They say they need it to take care of their sick mother. I hate when they do this repeatedly even when their mother is not sick." M-2.5-1 shared, "I do not like how people here lie. In the Middle East, I bought a car. The owner said it was a good car, and I looked at the car and it looked okay. I paid the deposit to the owner. I took the car to be inspected and learned that the engine did not work. I requested the owner refund my money to me but he refused." Two do not like how the hosts always borrow money. F-3.5-8 said, "I do not like how hosts often say they do not have money and ask people to borrow money. However, they do not ultimately return the money, though they may say they will." Three do not appreciate the host corruption. M-3-3 added, "I do not like the police. They accept bribes and are corrupt. They think Chinese are rich. When I first got here I had to give them money many times."

Others noted how they dislike interpersonal aspects of the host people. Three mentioned their dislike of how the host men treat them as women. F-3-5 said, "In Central Asia when walking on the road with other foreign women teammates, men will whistle at us or walk by us while we are walking and talk to us. I do not like this." Two do not like how the hosts communicate indirectly. F-6-6 said, "Hosts are polite and it is hard for them to refuse people. You invite them to your home to eat. Then she will think of reasons to say she cannot, but really she does not want to come. And when they are angry they will still smile." Two interviewees dislike how hosts are too concerned about their family's thoughts. F-8-10 said, "The families have strong control over others in the family. If someone becomes a believer, their family members exert pressure on them to not believe. It bothers me when the family exerts large pressure on others to follow their ideas." M-3-6 does not appreciate peoples' coldness in relationships. He said, "Many are enthusiastic towards you at first, but then they become cold. At first, they may say, 'You are my brother. I am your brother.' You think your relationship is great, but after a while, the relationship will change."

Some interviewees dislike aspects of the culture and people related to the hosts' work ethic. M-3-3 mentioned how hosts do not complete jobs. He said, "If you ask them to do something and you do not call them every day, they will not complete the work. When they do not complete it, if you get angry at them, they will quit the job and angrily say, 'I quit'. You cannot cause him to be angry. Otherwise, he will not complete it for you." Difficult for M-10-8 is the hosts' laziness. He said, "I do not like their laziness. They do everything slowly. Their laziness leads to them being poor. Their laziness affects their working efficiency and causes problems."

Also expressed were interviewees disliking how the hosts view foreigners. M-3-4 dislikes the unequal treatment towards Chinese. He said, "Host believers or nonbelievers give special treatment to people from America, Europe, and Japan, places that are most developed. I think people should be seen as equals." Two interviewees do not appreciate how the hosts have a reliance on others. M-8-11 said, "Their reliance on foreigners is too large. When they see a foreigner, they want to receive some benefit for themselves. I do not like this."

As for other aspects of the host culture and people that were disliked, F-6-6 does not like the inconvenient, unreliable, and slow public transportation. F-3-5 dislikes the prevalence of smokers in the Middle East.

Extent of Self-Disclosure with Hosts

In regards to whom the interviewees share with when they are frustrated, many (11 people) said they share with both host believers and host nonbelievers. Six interviewees mentioned sharing struggles with host believers, but not with host nonbelievers. Some only commented on sharing with host believers, but they did not mention anything about any sharing with nonbelievers.

Five interviewees explained how they do not share with any hosts when they have frustrations. M-8-11 said, "Usually I will share with other missionaries." M-3-4 said, "When I have struggles I share with Chinese leaders." As for reasons why people do not share their struggles with hosts, two did not want to show the hosts their weaknesses. M-10-8 said, "I rarely share struggles with host believers. We do not want to let them see our weaknesses and struggles." Two mentioned they do not share their struggles with hosts because the hosts will not understand them. M-8-5 said, "For sharing with host believers, our culture has differences so I do not share with them." F-3.5-8 does not share with hosts because Chinese understand her better. Because of his host language limitations, M-5-15 can only share struggles with those who speak English. M-3-6 shares with host nonbelievers, because he learned in a mission class to share struggles with host nonbelievers.

In summation of the missionaries' cross-cultural relationship experiences, there were multiple factors mentioned for building closer relationships. Eight of the interviewees listed helping one another. Also listed was the necessity of having sufficient language skills. Other common responses were being like them, cooking for them, and respecting and caring for them. On how the interviewees met their closest host friends, eight of them met them through teaching Chinese. Other common responses were that they were teammates or neighbors, or met in a host church or playing sports.

On what the interviewees most appreciate about the host culture and people, the most prevalent responses were their politeness, enthusiasm, hospitality, and respect for elders. Relevant aspects of the culture or people they dislike are that they are perceived as frequently telling lies and being deceptive or cheaters. Also mentioned were how the host men treat single missionary women, the corruption of the police, and hosts' indirectness in communication. Another question was if they shared their frustrations or struggles with hosts. Most of the respondents do share with host believers or nonbelievers. Five of the 25 respondents explained not sharing with host believers or nonbelievers. Discussing reasons interviewees do not share, some talked about how they do not want the host believers to see their weaknesses. Also stated was that the hosts would not understand the interviewees' struggles.

Host Language Ability

Of the 25 missionaries interviewed, three people studied language full-time for at least two years. F-6-4 learned Russian growing up and worked for a Russian company in China as a translator. M-8-5 and F-7-11 attended a host college for their bachelor's degree. M-8-5 continued for a master's degree there.

Of the 25 interviewees, nine people studied language part-time for at least two years; three people have studied full-time between six months and two years; seven people have studied part-time, between six months and two years; and, two of the interviewees studied less than six months. None of the interviewees only studied by themselves or did not study at all.

Language Levels

Subjects were asked about their language ability. For example, when asked, "Can you shop and go to a bank?" 21 people said "no problem." Four people said they had "some problems." M-3-3 said, "Yes for shopping, but not doing something at a bank." No one said they cannot do these tasks.

For the question, "Can you have casual conversation with hosts?" fifteen said "no problem." For example, M-4-7 said, "Basic conversation is proficient. I can talk about the weather, politics, or the news." M-8-11 said, "Yes, and discussing deeper topics is not a monumental challenge." Ten of the interviewees said they have "some problems" in conversing. F-13-7 said, "Yes, but if too complex of a topic I cannot." F-4-1 said, "I can understand when they are talking. Sometimes they cannot understand me. I can express simple topics, but I cannot talk about profounder matters." M-3-3 said he mostly uses English. He said, "When I speak the host language, I speak slowly. Most of my friends can speak English. I speak little of the host language, so I have learned the language slowly. At the orphanage, we speak English." None of the interviewees said they could not converse with hosts at all.

For the question "Can you read host language newspapers, etc.?" eight people said "no problem." F-8-10 said, "I can understand 70 percent of a newspaper. Sometimes I watch the host news and can understand most of it." Twelve of the interviewees said they have "some problems" in reading. Six people said they could not read anything.

As for the question of "Can you preach in the host language?" slightly less than half of those responding to the question said that they preached with "no problems" in the host language. M-9-10 said, "I have done this many times." Two people said "some problems" in preaching. Seven people said, "I cannot preach."

Summarizing this section on language learning, twelve of the 25 respondents had studied language part-time or full-time for at least two years. All respondents had taken at least some formal language school, and none had learned the language by only studying alone. For the questions asked them about their language abilities, it is important to clarify that their responses were according to their own perceptions of their ability, were not based on any tests, and may or may not be accurate to their true abilities. Some ambiguity exists from some of the interviewees' responses to the language questions. For example, though F-6-6 described herself as having "no problems" in conversing with hosts, she expressed elsewhere in the interview how she still has limitations in building relationships with hosts because of her language ability. Similar to this is M-4-13, who also said he has "no problems" in conversing with hosts, but he elsewhere in the interview said that sometimes when trying to make host friends, they have trouble understanding him talking to them.

Level of Comfort on the Field

Comfortable Experiences on the Field

When asked about when they have felt comfortable on the field, five people said because of hosts' friendships. F-6-4 said, "When we see them, we are ecstatic. When we have struggles, we share with them. When they have difficulties, they share with us. Sometimes we invite them to our home to eat or go to their house to eat. We have a tight relationship. I feel that though we are in a foreign country, they treat us as their relatives. They are like relatives or close friends to us. We do not feel lonely." F-5-2 said, "I love to be together with hosts, to hang out or eat together, or study the Bible with them. In all regards, including relationships with hosts, I feel content here."

Four people mentioned they are comfortable because the host culture is familiar to them. M-9-10 said, "I have been here nine years. I have many friends. I have host friends who are believers. Now my family is all here. For me, it is my home, here in Southeast Asia." F-5-3 said, "I can close my eyes and know where everything is. I can consider how when I first moved here, I did not understand anything, but now I can close my eyes and know where the coffee shop is. I know where that supermarket is. I feel like I am at my own home."

Four commented on the comfortable environment. F-4-1 said, "I like the scenery and clean air." M-4-7 said, "We go to a park to walk around. Sometimes we go fishing with others. We go climb mountains and have a barbecue on the mountain. These are all great."

Four noted their positive and enjoyable experiences with their team. M-2.5-1 said, "Our team can become not only co-workers but friends. When we have stress in our lives, we can share with one another and help each other. This helps me in carrying some of my stress." F-3-5 said, "I have a Chinese teammate here. We have been able to talk about everything going on in our lives, and our stresses here. We pray for each other and sing worship songs together. This has made me feel comfortable. We can talk through and resolve any conflicts we have."

Three noted how life on the mission field is less stressful for them. M-3-3 said, "I feel less stressed than when I was in China. The pace of life is slow. This leads to me feeling comfortable." F-3.5-8 said, "I have more free time than I had in China."

Two feel comfortable because they have adapted to life in the host culture. M-5-15 said, "Now I have lived here four years. I can love this country from the inside and accept this place. Even if there is confusion or injustice in this country, my heart is still here."

M-2.5-1 mentioned the blessing of seeing God's work. He said, "God has sent Middle Eastern refugees out of their own country, and many of them can receive the gospel. We go visit them three days a week. Some of them have come to the church and learned about God. Hearing believers' testimonies is encouraging for me. Though we meet difficulties with language and crossing cultures, we are encouraged by seeing how God is working here."

F-6-6 described how she enjoys her job. She said, "I am elated to be with children in a Muslim village. They respond well to my teaching. When they see that what you are teaching them can help them, they will change. I am delighted when I see them improve. My volunteer job in the village had numerous factors: teaching Chinese, painting, etc."

F-3-5 talked about how her life now is better, compared to the hardest time she had her first year on the field. She said, "My first year in Central Asia was so stressful and terrible. After that first year, I was completely burned out. I feel better now. I feel I am enjoying relationships, ministry, and language learning. After my experiences before, God has said to me 'I brought you here. I know all your worries.'"

Uncomfortable Experiences on the Field

Four have had difficulties in interpersonal relationships with hosts. F-3.5-8 said it is hard for her to trust hosts after her host friend stole her money. She said, "Because of my relationship with that girl and her stealing my money, it has been hard to trust any other hosts." F-8-10 does not like how the hosts will bother her about not being married. She said, "I do not like when people often ask me, 'Are you married?' Especially because I am older, I feel like people think 'Do you have some kind of problem or something?'"

Two mentioned difficulties with host police. F-4-1 said, "The police try to get money from Chinese. This causes me discomfort." M-5-15 said, "Once I was riding a motorbike and took an illegal turn. For people here, if they had the same violation they would have to pay one dollar to take care of it, but they wanted 50 dollars from me as a foreigner. I was furious. At that time I could not speak the language, and I spoke in English but the police could not understand."

Two feel distressed because of team conflicts. F-5-2 said, "It was hard to work together with my Korean leader. At that time I know he was discontented with me, which caused me even more pressure. These pressures lasted about two years, my first and second years in the Middle East. He wanted me to do more and more, which gave me even greater pressure." F-6-6 said, "Our team has problems that have not been solved over many years. It is problems between me and teammates, and conflicts between others. Most of our teammates are from Hong Kong, except me. We have over ten people."

Two noted difficulties with loneliness. M-3-3 said, "Being here alone makes me lonely. My main problem is not a lack of teammates, but rather that I want to be married." F-7-11 said, "Being here alone after teammates left was terrible and I felt lonely. It was awful."

Two have had difficulties with the environment. M-3-6 said, "This country is not beautiful from the outside. We are without places to help us release our stress. If we were not here for the purpose of the gospel, we would not have come to this country." F-7-11 said about the weather, "Southeast Asia is too humid. It negatively affects my body."

M-4-7 mentioned stress with his family. He said, "Sometimes my wife and I have arguments. We have life stressors that make us worried, like our children's education."

F-5-2 talked about ministry challenges. She said, "Last semester I realized I easily like to compare myself with others. This takes away much of my peace and contentment in ministry."

F-6-4 talked about challenges with medical care. She said, "The first time I came here I had health issues. I went to the hospital, but medical care is bad. It was impossible to solve my problem. When I went to have a child, I was told that not all hospitals here can allow foreigners to have babies. I could not find a hospital that would accept us. In addition, the first six months of my child's life, he was not able to get a checkup at the hospital."

A challenge for M-3-6 is inconvenience. He said, "We wanted to buy a car. For a foreigner to buy a car, we have to be approved by the government. We bought the car, but we had to register the car in our host friend's name. It was hard to find a friend who was willing to help us."

In conclusion, the most frequent response for what made them comfortable on the field (5 interviewees) was friendships with hosts. These people mentioned how they had mutually trusting and loving relationships with hosts. Four interviewees discuss their intimate and encouraging team, which was characterized by earnest prayer together and mutual spiritual encouragement. Other noteworthy responses were their familiarity with the place and the attractive environment. The most common response for experiences that made them uncomfortable was interpersonal relationship difficulties with hosts. Other relevant responses included the host police, loneliness, the weather, and team conflict.

Factors for Staying on the Field

As for the most critical factors for staying on the field, eleven interviewees mentioned the importance of God's calling of them. Two felt a call when they were young. M-2-2 said, "I have had this call since I was young. When I was young my mother and grandmother prayed to God for me and offered me to minister for God. I clearly remember how God moved in me when I was reading Acts 1:8 in the Bible. I then knew God's calling for me to be a missionary. My family supported me, especially my mother." M-3-4 describes the significance of his wife's calling to missions from when she was young. Five people said how God's calling has kept them on the field. M-8-5 said, "Seeing God's calling on you, you can persevere on the field. If your calling from God is unclear when you meet difficulties it will be easy to quit. Why are we still on the field? When God clearly gives us this calling, we will have the strength to continue." Three interviewees feel they are called to a certain task or ministry by God. M-9-10 said, "I know my task here. I cannot leave here. The reason I can persevere up to this point is God's calling." M-4-7 said, "I believe God called me to be here. I can understand that in my ministry I am providing valuable contributions. I have experience and can help co-workers. I can help host friends come to faith. I see that I am impacting peoples' lives." F-3.5-8 spoke of a certain calling she had to reach the peoples' souls. She said, "When I came to this place and saw all the people around me walking through a bazaar, my heart was broken for all the people around me who were lost and would go to hell when they died. I burst into tears and decided to stay here long-term. In times when I feel weak and have challenges and sadness, I know about God's calling to me to bring the gospel to these people."

Eleven noted how the spiritual needs of the host culture on the mission field were noteworthy contributors for keeping them there. Four mentioned the desire to see people saved on the field. F-4-1 said, "I have a burden for college students here to be saved and become God's disciples. Young people want to know God, but they do not know that only through Jesus can they know God." M-5-9 said, "In the villages here many souls have not heard the gospel. Remote villages have few Christians, and villages do not have any believers or a church." Four mentioned how a burden keeps them on the mission field. M-5-14 said, "I have considered leaving the field, because of visa issues. I am still here because I have a burden for the people. I like to be with them. When I pray for them, my heart is moved for them. If I stay for ten or more years and only one person has become a believer, it is all worthwhile." Three talked about another motivation of desiring to see flourishing host churches. F-3-5 said, "I want to see host believers have their own resources, that the host church can light a fire and develop the ministry on their own. This is the reason I want to be here long-term."

Seven interviewees talked about the importance of family support in keeping them on the field. Many noted their parents' support in steady prayer for them and encouragement. F-5-3 said, "My parents have supported me. They pray for me each day. When I have difficulties I can share with them, and they will pray for me." Three talked about family support from other family members. F-13-7 said,

> My family's support is key. When considering coming to Southeast Asia, the major factor holding me back was I was worried about my mother because her health was poor and she was old. At that time this was what caused me to be uneasy. You know how important our parents are to Chinese people. In fact, there is an old Chinese expression that says, especially with women, if you leave your parents you have not fulfilled your filial piety. This was hard for me, but the reason God could help me still come was that I had my sister taking care of my mother. My sister works at our church and is my chief supporter.

Others related similar support from family.

Two mentioned how, after initially leaving the field long-term, they moved back to that country several years later. M-5-15 said, "When I first came here, after a half a year, I wanted to leave. I did not like it here. I left the mission field, but God was constantly calling me and tugging at me. God lit a fire in my heart that started burning. I knew I wanted to return to this place to minister, even if I suffered or had difficulties." F-6-4 said, "When I was first here for four years, I had to return home early because of health problems, but I continued to have a burden for the place and miss friends here while I was back in China. Before I came back, I was nervous, but this burden and purpose never changed. If I did not have such a burden, I would not be here. I have a job at home and a house. Everything is easier there, including our children's education."

Two noted the importance of being trailblazers for Chinese missionaries. M-2.5-1 said, "We are the first generation of Chinese missionaries in the Middle East sent from Chinese house churches. Now we are stumbling about, but we hope to help the next generation of Chinese missionaries that come here, that they may avoid making some of the mistakes we have made." M-12-12 said, "I am a Chinese missionary. Chinese are not good at being missionaries. I want to become a Chinese missionary who is a flourishing missionary. Then I can help future generations of Chinese missionaries be effective. I am a trailblazer."

Two said how a love for the people keeps them there. F-13-7 said, "When I had been here five years, I was critical of this country and wanted to leave, but later I realized that a chief reason for what has kept me staying in this place has been my love for the people. I love everything here, so I think I could not leave." M-10-8 said, "Of course we do not enjoy life here as much as we do in China. This place in all regards is worse than China, but we are willing to stay, because of our love for the people."

F-6-6 mentioned the significance of God's guidance in her staying on the field. She said, "I am aware of how God has guided me. I have many times of wanting to go back to China. My home church wants me to go back and pressured me to go back, but after praying about it, I felt like God wanted me to stay here and minister. I have persevered."

F-7-11 talked about how a clear purpose keeps her on the field. She said, "Although I have had hesitations over the years to be here, my heart has been clear on God's purposes to be here. When I came, I knew that I planned to stay for ten years. I said this to myself when I got here, which has helped keep me on the field."

M-3-3 remains on the mission field out of a sense of obligation, as he has not been replaced yet. He said, "God has given me a task, but I have not completed it yet. I have not had anyone else come who can replace me in this work at the orphanage. No one has come to replace me, so I cannot leave."

Support Structures that Keep Them on the Field

Discussing support structures that keep them on the field, many mentioned their mission agency's support. Six noted comprehensive support from their international agency. F-4-1 said, "I have support from my mission agency. I receive support from other Chinese or foreigners in our mission agency. They encourage my heart and pray for me. We often see our mission agency leader who lives in China. We share with one another. Our on-the-field agency leaders help me too." M-4-7 said, "The mission agency's support has been huge. The mission agency established and oversees a language center here, which has been a great ministry platform for me. We have become friends with our teammates and can minister together. When I have difficulties or other needs, my teammates or others in our agency can help me, like with moving homes or taking care of our children's education." F-7-11 said,

> When I ministered together with on-field [international mission agency] leaders, they did not just tell me what to do, but they guided me in being involved in their ministry. In anything related to ministering among the hosts, they asked me 'What do you think is the best way to do it?' Those overseeing us on the field wanted us to learn how to think about life on the mission field, rather than us simply doing everything they tell us to do.

Others expressed how international agencies assist primarily with finances and other needs, rather than with guidance on ministry. M-5-9 said, "Our mission agency helps us with finances. Our mission agency leaders have told us they have never been on the mission field, so with ministry, they cannot help us considerably. Sometimes they will come to a city to give a class, and I will go meet them to do the class. I often contact and pray with some missionaries from our mission agency."

F-5-2 said she does not receive significant support from her international agency. She said, "I do not have consistent contact with my mission agency. I think I do not need this support from the mission agency leader as much anymore."

As for those within Chinese mission agencies, four said they receive comprehensive support from the Chinese agency. M-10-8 said, "The mission agency supports us with managing our finances and taking care of all of our administrative tasks. They help us make plans that we tell them, to let them hold us accountable for those plans. Every Friday we contact our leader. We have stable missionary care through small groups." M-4-13 said, "Our mission agency leaders try to understand our situations and pray for us. Our organization's training has benefited us. They help us with finances. These all contribute to us staying here."

Others talk of spiritual support and teaching from their Chinese agency. M-2-2 said, "Our spiritual support has been through our mission agency. Our leader weekly gives us classes online. This is a way they have supported us. Our leader shares Scriptures with us and encourages us." F-4-9 added, "With some of our organization's leaders when I am angry I can speak to them honestly. They can provide an objective perspective on our situation. This is important." F-6-4 said, "Our mission leaders have regular teaching online. We learn teambuilding, being a leader, and building relationships. This teaching facilitates us constantly improving and thinking about our lives here. What we learn, we will use. This helps give us fresh strength."

Ten interviewees talked of the support they receive from churches in China. Seven of these have received comprehensive support from their home church, and this contributes to keeping them on the field. F-5-3 said, "My home church as a whole will pray for us twice per month. I have other friends at the church who pray for us every week at their small group meetings. I often talk to them and send them my prayer letter. During the Chinese New Year, they send me gifts. I can sense they care for us. They feel like my family. Even while I have been living far away, they have not forgotten me."

Three mentioned how they were encouraged by older people at their home church. F-4-9 said, "Last year when we went home, the old women in the house church in the village sat and listened to us share all day. Then they all prayed for us. This is a huge support that helps us remain here until now. We have backup support." Two interviewees talked about how they have regular contact with someone in the church and someone from the church has visited. M-3-4 said, "Our supporting church always prays for and encourages us and financially supports us. We talk once or twice a month. They have come before to see us."

Three noted how they receive all forms of support from many churches in China. F-3-5 said, "Now my support comes from several churches. Their concern and care for me have helped me realize this is God's work and not my own. Now several churches in China care for me, personally and financially."

Six talked about how support from their home church is primarily financially and with prayers. M-2.5-1 said, "Our church that adopted us financially supports us and prays for us."

M-3-3 said he would be embarrassed to the churches in China if he did not complete his work. He said, "Churches in China support me to be here and work. This work has not been completed. I would feel embarrassed to churches in China if I did not complete my task here."

Three missionaries were essentially independent of support from a mission agency or home church. M-8-5 said, "We rarely talk to our home church. Our mission leaders give us pressure and we rarely talk to them. We have teammates but do not know them well. We are on our own here." M-3-6 said, "This Spring Festival we went home. Our home church did not want us to return to the mission field. This has been hard. We receive little shepherding or missionary care from our home church. In addition, we do not belong to a mission agency." M-5-9 said, "Now I do not have any support from teammates. I live in a village. I do not receive any support from China."

Seven commented on how teammates' support helps keep them on the field. F-3.5-8 said, "If I were here alone, I would not persevere, but I have a team. My teammates care for me. I am not alone." Similarly, F-3-5 said, "Very important has been teammates' support. If my team were not all working together well, it would be hard and I would have left long ago." M-10-8 said his relationship with his teammates is one of ministering with them and supporting each other. He said, "Our teammates support us. We all pray for and comfort each other, and minister together. We can all be responsible for each other in staying here. We see each other a few times a week." Some noted sharing with their teammates. F-4-1 said, "My team encourages me. I can share with them everything going on with me."

Also mentioned by four interviewees for keeping them on the field is mentors' support. Two note a mentor from their mission agency. F-5-3 said, "There is a woman in our agency who is my leader, and we have a tight relationship. She is like a mentor to me. Twice a month we talk to each other on a video. She is a missionary, so she understands our challenges on the mission field.'" F-3.5-8 said, "My mentors give me suggestions. I contact them once a month."

F-8-10 commented on how her psychological counselor has given her support. She said, "This counselor helps me see aspects in my heart. If I did not have this kind of counselor, it would be hard. She is an experienced missionary, so she gives me suggestions and assistance. She tells me where I have done wrong, and what I need to be careful about on the field."

Three described support from other Chinese friends. M-4-7 said how friends have come to visit. He said, "We keep in touch with each other and they pray for us. They will come to see us about twice a year." F-5-2 gets support from Chinese missionaries in other countries. She said, "I have a close friend in another country, in Southeast Asia. She is a missionary and has been for many years. We can help and support each other greatly."

Three people talked about how encouraging large mission conferences are to them. F-3-5 said, "At large mission conferences we can meet people ministering in other places and encourage one another. This shows me that I am not alone here and that God is working in different places."

F-5-2 has been encouraged to stay on the field through reading books. She said, "Reading books has encouraged me. The most helpful was a book written by the English Puritan Richard Baxter that was written in the 1600s. This aided me in having a new vision. I could see God's majesty. I realized I needed to wait for God and see his unspeakable beauty. This helps me keep in perspective my challenges here."

M-9-10 mentioned how short-term teachers and teams encourage him. For teachers, he said, "Teachers will come to teach and encourage us. We do this every three months. We study a course, and they encourage us with God's words. I have received shepherding from these teachers." And about short-term mission teams, M-9-10 said, "I take short-term mission trip teams from China around to all the places here where I minister. They can see what I am doing. They come once a year and these are encouraging for us." F-7-11 said, "Mainland Chinese come to do short-term trips and encourage us."

On-Field Support that Workers Wish they Had Received

As for on-field support the interviewees wish they had received but have not, ten missionaries express the need for someone experienced in missions in their mission agency to guide them or someone to give them missionary care. Some interviewees talk about how they lack mentors who can guide them in solving problems. F-5-2 said, "Many missionaries like myself have difficulties the first couple of years on the field. It would be valuable to have a mentor who can give us practical assistance, guidance or counseling. The missionary could talk to this mentor to get help when any difficulties come up."

M-4-13 said, "We do not have an experienced person to help us with ministry. Our Chinese mission agency leaders do not understand our lives here." M-5-9 commented on how his mission agency is in the early stages and inexperienced. He said, "Our agency is relatively young, and has only existed for about ten years. None of us in this country have extensive experience. Our needs on the field are to have a mission mentor." M-12-12 said, "We have situations here that we have not experienced, and we do not know what to do, like in sharing the gospel with people. We do not have a mentor. All of our mission agency leaders are in China and do not understand life here."

Some interviewees mention a desire for the mission agency to have a fixed person to help them when they have difficulties. M-4-7 said, "Sometimes when I talk to leaders of the mission agency about our lives and ministry here, they do not understand everything I am telling them, which is disappointing for me. I wish we had a set and consistent person, who had extensive cross-cultural mission experience and could help us and give us a model to follow and tell us what to do." M-3-4 said, "We lack member care. We do not have a fixed person who we can talk to when we have problems. It would be beneficial to have someone else besides our main leader who can care for us. When we meet problems we do not know who to talk to or how to solve them."

Other interviewees noted other needs related to lacking missionary care. M-3-3 being single needs more missionary care. He said, "Because I am a single man I will feel lonely sometimes. I wish I had someone to care for me. Now I do not have this on the field, so I often feel lonely." M-9-10 said he lacks being cared for on the field. He said, "I have not had anyone shepherding me on the field. When I have had culture shock I have not known with whom to share my struggles. I do not have anyone to share with and am without anyone who cares for me. I think if I had this, it would have released some of my stress."

F-8-10 thinks that international agencies do not always know how to care for Chinese missionaries. She said, "Sometimes international mission agencies do not know how to give Chinese missionaries member care. Doing member care for Chinese missionaries is a new concept."

Another prevalent response to the question about on-field support the interviewees lack is the need for more financial support. Nine people mentioned needing more financial support. M-3-3 talked about inconsistent support from China. He said, "We have to rely on support from China. They give us money once every three months, but sometimes they wait four or five months before they give us money. This is not reliable." M-8-11 talked about how their financial support from churches in China is insufficient.

Four expressed how it is stressful when supporters cut off support. F-3.5-8 said, "Sometimes supporters will cut off their support, which is stressful for me. If I see my account is near being empty, it is hard." M-8-5 said, "When our supporting church has problems, they cannot support us anymore. This is stressful." F-6-4 said, "Because of recent security issues in China, we have had less contact with our home church, and sometimes our financial support cuts off, which is a challenge." F-3-5 said, "In my first year I often had financial difficulties. Even for a while, I was without having any salary, because people who previously supported me discontinued supporting me."

Four people said they lack adequate financial support for their children's educational costs. M-8-11 said, "We do not have enough money for our child's education, so we need to resolve it on our own." M-8-5 said, "Our child will need to go to school, but we do not have financial support to do this. This is stressful." M-2.5-1 said, "We worry about money for our son's school. The support we receive from China is inadequate for everything we need. We do not have any special money allocated for our son." M-10-8 added, "Our support for living costs is deficient. We have great stress and worries about my daughter's tuition as we do not know where the child's tuition money will come from."

As for those seeking to earn money on the field to provide for themselves, M-12-12 said it was hard to make any profit when doing business. He said, "It is hard to do business here. I have opened several businesses and with all of them, I have lost money. Last year my business went bankrupt, and we lost considerable money. Because the school I lead now is free, we do not make a profit. We have had outsiders who financially support our businesses." M-8-5 mentioned how he is looking for a new job to try to self-support because support from China is scarce. He said, "Financially we are stressed. Usually, a church in China will give us money, but it is a small amount. I am trying to find a job here. I had a job but it was not a proper fit. I am looking for a job again."

Three people mentioned how ongoing support they need on the field is to have more people come. They need like-minded teammates to come and share the load. M-9-10 said, "It is important to have a teammate who can be of one mind with me." Similarly, M-2.5-1 said, "We need a teammate who can share the load with us. Sometimes I do feel lonely because of this. We need people who will not just do what I plan for them to do, but people who can help share the load of leadership with me."

In concluding this section on key factors for people staying on the field, the most widespread response was that it is God's calling that keeps them there. Also noteworthy is their family's support as well as having an understanding of the needs on the field. Also mentioned were having a burden for the people, and desiring to be trailblazers for Chinese missionaries.

Discussing support structures most relevant in keeping the missionaries on the field, many talked about the comprehensive support they receive from their international mission agency, including providing management of finances, a mentor, training, member care, guidance, and a tight-knit team on the field. Some belong to an international agency but have very little contact with their agency leaders or any teammates. With those belonging to Chinese mission agencies, some have also noted from their mission agency similar wide-ranging support. Others belong to a Chinese mission agency but have received little member care or guidance in their ministry from their agency. Several missionaries have talked about the significant all-encompassing spiritual, financial, and relational support they receive from their home church, or from other churches in China. Others have had a home church assigned to them through their mission agency, and may only receive prayer and financial support from them. Also of note for multiple interviewees was support they receive from their teammates or from mentors in their agency. A few of the interviewees are independent missionaries not connected closely to a mission agency, churches in China, or teammates on the field.

In answering the question of on-field support they wish they had received, but have not, the most widespread response was to have an experienced person in the agency who can guide them in ministry and someone who can provide missionary care. Another noteworthy response was lacking sufficient financial support. Some wish they could work and be self-supporting. For others, it is stressful when supporters cut off support. Some have insufficient support to cover the costs of their children's education.

Other Positive or Negative Experiences

Positive Experiences

As for other positive experiences, four noted their close friendships with teammates on the mission field. F-4-1 said, "I like having friends with whom I can share. When I moved here, I knew it would be important to have friends that I could openly share with, to release some of the stress that comes with living here. With my teammates and other friends, when I feel sad or difficulties arise, I can share openly with them. This helps me." M-3-3 said, "Sometimes when we eat together with our teammates, we encourage each other, and I feel great." F-13-7 said, "My teammates and I prop each other up and bless each other." F-7-11 said, "Since many people left a couple of years ago, a family has come and two Chinese families have come. I have been able to help them and minister with them."

Three of the interviewees mentioned seeing God's work in their lives. M-2.5-1 said, "Previously we faced financial stress, but every time we face these problems, I will pray for God's guidance. Through meeting these difficulties we can learn to look towards God and to not complain. God will help us during the most difficult times." F-6-6 said, "I have seen how God has helped me grow up and mature on the field. After I came here I faced difficulties and setbacks, but now I have grown spiritually. I have had experiences and have matured."

Three described positive experiences in ministry. F-6-4 said, "Last summer we did a summer camp in a host middle school. We worked together with short-term workers from Taiwan to do the summer camp. It was an amazing experience." M-4-7 said, "Seeing a host Muslim friend be interested in Christianity has been encouraging." M-8-11 said, "I see the ministry we are doing now. We are progressing and growing."

M-3-4 talked about helping others financially. He said, "We have learned, though sometimes we do not have much money, to financially support others in need. God can minister to other people through us."

PRESENTATION OF FINDINGS

Negative Experiences

Some mentioned negative experiences related to their mission agency or team. Four mentioned team challenges. F-13-7 explained her teammate's problems. She said, "My teammate's depression led her to begin psychologically attacking me. It was a hard period, and we made her return to China. These attacks lasted about a year. I was depressed then, but at that time our leader helped and encouraged me, and said it was not my own problem but hers." Two talked about their mission leaders' misunderstandings of them. M-9-10 talked about misunderstandings from his home agency. He said, "Sometimes Chinese missionaries will say spiritual words like 'Let God take care of it' if the family back home has problems. If a mission agency leader encourages the missionaries like this, and the missionary's parents are sick but the missionary does not go see his parents, this is terrible." F-5-2 mentioned people leaving constantly. She said, "Each year I have a period which is lower. Our agency sends people here who stay for two or three years and then go back. We are already tight with them, get along well, and minister happily together. Then after a year or two, they leave. People are always leaving and new people are coming. Every year I experience these challenging circumstances."

Three people commented on physical problems they have had. F-4-1 said how the food negatively affects her body. She said, "Because food here lacks nutrition, I have had physical challenges. This is a challenge. Sometimes I have to go back to China. Sometimes I am too tired also because of the stress of language learning." M-3-6 talked about their infertility. He said, "Every family here has many children and they often ask us why we do not have children. Though we have been married several years, we have not been able to have children. This is stressful." F-6-6 said team conflict hurt her body. She said, "Team problems have affected my health. I have not known how to respond when people say words that hurt me. So I have kept bitterness in my heart, as I have been unwilling to resolve our problems. After a while, I had health problems and did not want to eat. I could not sleep and was unhappy. Some of these bad experiences have affected my health."

Two shared of their negative experiences in language learning. M-2.5-1 talked how he considered leaving the field because of lacking language ability. He said, "Sometimes I feel frustrations, as I have to start all over with language learning. This is hard. Sometimes this is stressful. Sometimes we doubt our own calling. Does God really want us here? When I am frustrated, I will say, 'God. I do not have this language learning ability', and I think of excuses." M-3-4 is frustrated because of not progressing in language. He said, "Now we are in our third year here. I wish that our language was better now, but our first couple of years we split time between ministry and language learning. I wish when we got here we would have first studied language full-time for a while, instead of doing part-time."

As for other negative experiences shared by the interviewees, M-12-12 talked about some Chinese missionaries who should not be on the field, and how they negatively impact other missionaries. M-3-3 talked about depression and loneliness. He said, "For a while I felt low. I did not want to talk to people or be with people. I was homesick and wanted to move home. Each year I feel like this several times and feel discouraged. I do not want to go out but to stay alone by myself. I feel depressed at those times. It would be great if during these periods I had someone who could reach out to me to talk together on video. I would be excited." M-3-6 talked about his home church's lack of support. He said, "Our home church did not support us. This was a hard time. We are constantly thinking about this. We have also considered going back to China. We did not want to come back to the Middle East. Life here is hard. We have been in a valley recently." M-2.5-1 said difficulties exist in exchanging Chinese currency in the Middle East to the host currency. F-5-2 shared about feeling less connected with friends from China. M-2.5-1 talked about conflict with his wife. He said, "Sometimes when I argue with my wife, it gets intense, but we do not want people to know. If we let other believers here know, they will feel discouraged. They will say, 'How can missionaries be like this?' So my wife and I talk through problems and solve them on our own. Sometimes we feel heavy stress and want to leave the field."

In concluding this section on other positive or negative experiences the interviewees desired to share, the most prevalent positive response was seeing God's work. Also mentioned were friendships with teammates on the field and being encouraged by the ministry. Common negative experiences they desired to share included team difficulties, physical problems, leaders misunderstanding them, and challenges with language learning.

5

Analysis of Findings

THIS CHAPTER IN THE dissertation follows this outline: It first will present the emerging themes from the research, which is the main part of the chapter. This includes implications and interaction with the precedent literature. Second, implications will be drawn from the study.

Research Questions

The first research question addressed how Chinese cross-cultural workers have succeeded or struggled in cross-cultural relationships. It examined the prevailing impression of Chinese cross-cultural workers having difficulty in cross-cultural communication. Also of relevance for the study was analyzing how these Chinese cross-cultural workers adapted in learning the host language and assimilating to the host culture. Finally, the research investigated perceived factors that contributed to the more thriving Chinese cross-cultural workers developing effective cross-cultural relationships on the mission field. Research subjects included only those who have remained on the field for at least two years and did not return home prematurely.

The second research question in this research analyzed what pre-field and on the field experiences have contributed to Chinese cross-cultural workers' retention in cross-cultural service. This encompassed what pre-field preparation or on the field support has been useful to Chinese missionaries, and what kinds of pre-field preparation or on the field support they wish they had received, but did not. Also analyzed is what support structures (e.g. home church support, teammates' support, mission agency) or other specific factors have contributed to the missionaries' retention.

Emerging Themes

From the data reported in Chapter 4, twelve themes emerged. These included: how finances are a significant challenge; the need for vocational training; the impact of filial piety on Chinese missionaries; how there is no correlation between educational achievement and cross-cultural effectiveness; host language learning successes and struggles; how missionary preparation contributes to cross-cultural effectiveness; building intimate relationships with hosts; the mission team being a help and hindrance; the level of supportiveness of mission agencies; unique challenges for single missionaries; challenges of overcoming hosts' stereotypes and prejudices of Chinese; and, short-term missions being a helpful missionary preparation.

Finances are a Significant Challenge

Lack of finances is an obstacle for many of the Chinese missionaries. Those belonging to international mission agencies did not specify from where they received their financial support. For those within Chinese mission agencies, many noted how they received financial support from their home church in China, or from a church in China that their mission agency had introduced to them. Some mentioned receiving financial support from multiple churches in China. Many interviewees mentioned the inconsistent support they have received from churches in China. These challenges are very existential. Some interviewees noted stress in their marriage as a result of a lack of finances. In addition, finances are a basic need, because if they do not have adequate financial resources they must move back to China. These Chinese missionaries with unsteady financial support may be more likely to leave the field prematurely, which corresponds with what Rob Hay wrote in the ReMAP II study about higher retention of missionaries being produced by mission agencies that provide steady financial support.[1] Many other interviewees added that financial support from China is insufficient to provide for them and their family. These Chinese missionaries' challenges are consistent with the findings of Howard Brant that "sustainable finances" is the chief hindrance for majority world missions.[2]

Several Chinese missionaries described the stress that happens when their financial support is cut off. Stress occurred for these interviewees

1. Hay, "Finances," 339.
2. Brant, "Seven Essentials," 50.

when their financial supporters discontinued supporting them, either because of their house church in China being under Chinese government scrutiny or for other reasons. These missionaries' experiences parallel what Lim wrote how some NSC missionaries have challenges because financial aid from their home country is cut off.[3]

Several Chinese missionaries voiced a concern about lack of financial support to cover their children's education. These missionaries did not receive any funds specifically allocated for their children's education from their supporters in China, so they did not know from where the money for their children's education would come. These Chinese missionaries' challenges correspond to Lim's description of children's education being an overlooked financial support need for NSC missionaries.[4] Also relevant for mission agencies sending Chinese missionaries is Lane's advice that mission agencies and missionaries need to clarify who will pay for what on the field, including children's education.[5]

One interviewee explained the inconvenience in exchanging Chinese currency that he received from house churches in China into the host currency in the Middle East. He must exchange the money he receives from Chinese churches first from Chinese Yuan to U.S. dollars, and then from U.S. dollars to the host currency; he is unable to directly convert Chinese Yuan to the host currency at host banks in the Middle East. His challenges in exchanging his Chinese money directly into the host currency parallel Denis Lane's findings on the difficulty of missionaries from some countries exchanging their home country currency for the host currency.[6] In addition, this interviewee's challenges in exchanging money contribute to his overall lack of funds, as he loses money each time he exchanges money for another currency.

Need for Vocational Training

The second emerging theme from the findings was how the missionaries' lack of receiving vocational training hindered them. The interviewees' stated motivations for their concerns included that such skills or training would enable them to obtain a visa, have credibility on the field, meet host people,

---

3. Lim, "Finances," 342.
4. Lim, "Finances," 341.
5. Lane, *Tuning God's New Instruments*, 52.
6. Lane, *Tuning God's New Instruments*, 54.

and earn a profit on the field so as to assuage their financial challenges. A recurring theme throughout the interviews was peoples' lack of preparation in the area of vocational skills that would have enabled them to obtain a long-term visa and earn an income on the mission field. Responding about pre-field preparation they wish they had received but did not, eleven people talked about how what they were devoid of in preparation but needed was vocational training. 44 percent of interviewees mentioned this as compared to only 16 percent for the second most received response, revealing its significance and relevance for Chinese missionaries. Some added that vocational training would provide a platform and position in the society. Interviewees talked about the impossibility of remaining long-term on the field with a student visa, and how receiving vocational training is necessary for serving on the field long-term. Having a real job on the field is necessary so as to avoid the hosts being suspicious of the interviewees and their family and wondering from where they receive their money. These Chinese missionaries' challenges of lacking vocational training to use on the field correspond with what Seth Anyomi wrote about how majority world missionaries would benefit from pre-field vocational development training so that they might have a job on the mission field.[7]

Some of the interviewees discussed how vocational training would facilitate them finding a job, earning money, and providing for themselves and for their family. One interviewee noted the challenge of being able to earn a sufficient income through business to provide for his family, especially when receiving low support from China. Another interviewee added that it would be ideal to work and earn money on the mission field so he could meet more hosts and be freed from needing to worry about low financial support from China. These Chinese missionaries' desire to have jobs, receive an income, and be financially independent of unreliable financial support from house churches in China reinforces Chang's recommendation that low financial support can be overcome by sending "tentmakers," who work full-time on the mission field.[8]

Impact of Filial Piety on Chinese Missionaries

The third emerging theme for the Chinese missionaries is how filial piety in the Chinese society positively or negatively influences the missionaries' lives

7. Anyomi, "Mission Agency Screening," 236.
8. Chang, "Overcoming Low Financial Support," 354.

on the field. Analyzing in greater depth the various dynamics of filial piety that greatly impact Chinese missionaries, filial piety is defined in the classics and in popular thought as "support, subordination (or obedience), and continuing the family line."[9] Under the influence of Confucian values, filial piety involves the responsibilities of younger generations providing support for their parents, and "harmonizing family relations and maintaining family continuity."[10] In addition, "failure to live up to local standards of filial piety can result in damage to one's own self-image, to loss of reputation in the community, and to loss or diminution of one's inheritance."[11] This is why it can be shameful for Chinese missionaries when they move to the mission field if they are perceived as abandoning their aging parents in China and failing to live up to their society's standards of filial piety.

In most of East Asia today the family may be the primary resource to provide for the elderly.[12] A reason for this, particularly within the Mainland China context, is that there is a lack of financial provision from the government and reliable and affordable nursing home options for the elderly. An added factor for many of these Chinese missionaries is that as a result of being born during the era of Mainland China's "one-child policy," many of these Chinese missionaries are their parent's only child and do not have siblings to help provide for aging parents. This is the context that these missionaries are coming from. So it is no surprise that for many Chinese missionaries caring for parents is a major concern and potential contributor to missionary attrition.

This is reflected in statements made by interviewees. For example, a missionary expressed how, though she had an aging mother in China, she was able to go on the mission field, because her sister took the responsibility to take care of their mother. If her sister had not been willing to take care of their mother, the interviewee would have had a guilty conscience moving to Southeast Asia, feeling that she had abandoned her mother in China. This is a pertinent issue for Chinese missionaries in a similar situation, as their sense of obligation to take care of aging parents can prevent them from initially moving onto the field, or force them to leave the mission field earlier than they may desire. These circumstances are a major burden for these missionaries who have these experiences.

9. Ikels, "Introduction," 3.
10. Lai, "Filial Piety, Caregiving Appraisal, and Caregiving Burden," 205.
11. Ikels, "Introduction," 6.
12. Ikels, "Introduction," 9.

Many Chinese missionaries interviewed noted other positive and negative factors related to their family. Seven of the Chinese missionaries interviewed mentioned how their families' support was one of the principal influences for them staying on the field. Four of the respondents explained how both parents are Christians and support them through their steady prayers and encouragement. Three of the respondents talked about how support they receive from family is not necessarily only from their two parents, but rather from their sister, their brother, or from both their parents and extended family who are all Christians and all supportive of them being on the mission field. This factor is significant because it contributes to what leads these interviewees to initially become missionaries, and also to what keeps them on the field.

On the other hand, F-3-5 shared how her family's lack of support has been difficult for her. She said, "My parents have disapproved of me being on the mission field. [One reason is that] I [am] single. My mother and grandmother are believers, but my mother has also opposed me going." Family blessing is a large force and motivation for Chinese missionaries if their family is supportive. However, because of their filial piety context, their family's lack of support is equally difficult and hampering for them, as was expressed and experienced by F-3-5. How filial piety and the extent of their family's support contributes to or hinders these Chinese missionaries' retention on the field coincides with what Sarah Hay wrote about how family blessing is essential for NSC missionary retention, particularly in places where filial piety is significant.[13] In addition, Hung confirms how filial piety is important in Chinese society.[14] Lack of family support of their moving to the mission field can hinder such people from becoming missionaries, or force them to prematurely leave the mission field.

No Correlation between Educational Achievement and Cross-Cultural Effectiveness

The fourth emerging theme from the research is that there is no correlation between educational achievement and cross-cultural effectiveness. Of the 25 Chinese missionaries interviewed, eleven had no more than a middle or high school education. From this research, and from my personal judgment and evaluation of the missionaries through the interviews, no clear distinction in

---

13. Hay, "Selection: What it Means," 71.
14. Hung, "Filial Piety and Missionary Calling," 78.

effective cross-cultural adjustment was identifiable on the field for those with more formal school education compared to those with less. Many with only a middle school education seemed to flourish in learning the host language and building cross-cultural relationships, while some who had bachelor's degrees did not adjust as well in cross-cultural ministry.

These findings are contrary to Rob Hay's description that high retaining mission agencies have twice as many missionaries with master's or doctoral degrees.[15] These findings thus reveal a distinctive of the Chinese mission movement that is dissimilar to the Korean mission movement, which according to Park was partly successful because of the Korean mission movement's emphasis on formal education.[16] However, the discoveries of this research correlate with Jaap Ketelaar's findings that, though in general educated missionaries are more efficient cross-culturally on the mission field, some effective missionaries have received little formal school education.[17] These less formally educated Chinese missionaries' effectiveness in cross-cultural adjustment on the mission field is similar to what Nathaniel Abimbola in Nigeria described—that missionaries with his mission agency were effective on the field although most of them lacked education beyond middle school.[18] It is worth noting that the educational system in China is not the same as the U.S. educational system. So what a bachelor's degree means in the U.S. is not exactly what it means in China. For example, study at a university is much less common than in the United States and many Western countries.

Host Language Learning Successes and Struggles

A fifth emerging theme from the research is related to the interviewees' successes and struggles in learning the host language. For the purpose of this dissertation, I am considering proficiency in the host language to be being proficient in these abilities: reading the newspaper, going shopping, and conversing on daily kinds of issues. Using these parameters, eight of the 25 interviewees were proficient in the language. This level of "proficiency" may be most similar to Level 3 (General Professional Proficiency)

---

15. Hay, "Education," 55.
16. Park, "Missionary Movement of the Korean Church," 169.
17. Ketelaar, "Education," 58.
18. Abimbola, "Is Higher Education Required," 62.

of the Interagency Language Roundtable (ILR) scale (Interagency Language Roundtable).

Seven interviewees noted that sufficient language ability is paramount for making close host friends. Of the 25 interviewees, twelve studied the host language part-time or full-time in a class or with a tutor for at least two years, and all interviewees studied language part-time or full-time for at least six months. This reveals that language learning is a priority for all of these Chinese missionaries and the mission agencies that sent them. Eight of the interviewees, based on self-assessment of their host language abilities, were proficient in both conversing with hosts and reading fluently in the host language.

Ten of the interviewees responded that adjusting to the language was a significant challenge during their first years on the field. Some interviewees noted that having language deficiencies can be a barrier to making host friends. One interviewee expressed that in her first years on the field she had difficulty making closer relationships with hosts because her language was insufficient. Some interviewees shared that, at times, they desired to talk to hosts and make friends with them, but the hosts were able to understand what they were saying. One interviewee described how he can only self-disclose his struggles to hosts who speak English competently, as his host language is too poor to share in that language. Other interviewees described frustration because of lack of progress in the host language after being on the field multiple years, and one even talked about how he has considered leaving the mission field because of this struggle.

The impact of these interviewees' host language proficiency on their ability to make close host friends corresponds with both Christian and secular scholars who agree on the significance of learning the foreign language well in order to have effective cross-cultural relationships.[19]

How Missionary Preparation Contributes to Cross-Cultural Effectiveness

An additional emerging theme from the research was how missionary preparation contributes to cross-cultural effectiveness. All of the Chinese missionaries interviewed received some missionary preparation. This

---

19. Gudykunst and Hammer, "Strangers and Hosts," 126; Lingenfelter and Mayers, *Ministering Cross-Culturally*, 17; Moreau et al., *Effective Intercultural Communication*, 77–78; Elmer, *Cross-Cultural Servanthood*, 66, 77–78.

missionary preparation might have included English language acquisition; taking short-term mission trips to reach minority groups in China; attending a seminary for theological education; or, other forms of "mission training."

Nine interviewees had over two years of missionary preparation. Those who seemed to flourish most cross-culturally and have been on the mission field at least ten years, M-12-12 and F-13-7, received over two years of missionary preparation. By flourish, I mean they have succeeded in learning the language, developed friendships with the hosts, and seem to be living happy and fulfilled lives. F-13-7 received her MDiv in the U.S. In contrast, some missionaries belonged to international agencies that only provided three months of mission training without any specific theological education. However, from my own analysis and perception based on ten years of working in China, some of these missionaries still appeared to similarly flourish on the mission field. Conversely, some interviewees had over two years of missionary preparation but still seemed to struggle cross-culturally. This being the case, in this study, there was no clear correlation between receiving at least one year of missionary preparation and maintaining higher missionary retention, as was proposed by Blocher.[20]

Of the 25 Chinese interviewed, 24 of them received mission training. This "mission training" includes subjects such as: cultural differences in the host country; managing culture shock; language learning methods; adapting on the field; team dynamics; one's personal relationship with God; how God views missions; how to live on the field if one is single or married; stress management; and, better knowing the gospel. Again, those who had been on the field at least five years and had at least one year of mission training seemed to have superior cross-cultural understanding, adaptation, and prowess on the field. Nonetheless, there were also some missionaries that seemed to struggle cross-culturally, even having received extensive mission training. In addition, some missionaries only received three months of mission training but seemed to flourish building cross-cultural relationships and adjusting on the field. These realities reveal how inconclusive the findings were on whether receiving more extensive mission training contributed to Chinese missionary retention, as was proposed by Rob Hay that mission agencies with higher retention have two or three times higher requirements for mission training.[21]

20. Blocher, "ReMAP I," 18.
21. Hay, "Education," 55.

Thirteen of the missionaries received mission training but lacked formal theological education. Some of those who belonged to international agencies that offered three months of mission training but no theological education; they had been on the mission field at least five years, seemed cross-culturally savvy, and had close host friends. Only one of the 25 interviewees was deficient of mission training. The importance of pre-field mission training for the interviewees corresponds with what Rob Hay wrote how pre-field mission training is the most beneficial training for missionary retention in cross-cultural service.[22]

Twelve of the 25 Chinese interviewees received theological education. Seven of these had at least one year. When analyzing those who have been on the field at least five years, those with at least one year of prior theological education appeared to flourish more. On the other hand, there were also many interviewees sent through international mission agencies that did not provide pre-field theological education. Many of these missionaries, although they did not receive pre-field theological education, still seemed to flourish on the field. However, six of the 25 interviewees mentioned how theological education was helpful pre-field preparation for them. In addition, three others noted how theological education was a pre-field preparation they wish they had received, but did not. So it seems there were some parallels between the interviewees' experiences and Rob Hay's conclusions that missionaries in high retention agencies have twice as much theological education as those in low retention agencies.[23]

Building Intimate Relationships with Hosts

Another emerging theme from the research was the interviewees' successes and challenges in effectively building relationships with the hosts. In this dissertation, a person would be considered to have good relations if they had: extensive relationships with hosts, evidence of mutual trust, and a comfort level in socializing with hosts. Using these terms, most of the people seemed to be evidencing positive relationships with hosts. As was mentioned in the literature review, there are certain factors that generally are considered to be important for effectively building cross-cultural relationships. We see those factors reflected in a number of ways in the ability of these Chinese missionaries being able to adjust. One of these factors is

22. Hay, "Preparation Time," 105.
23. Hay, "Preparation Time," 106.

managing anxiety and uncertainty. Gudykunst and Kim write how when we communicate with those of other ethnic groups, we experience increased anxiety.[24] Having less anxiety and uncertainty results in superior "perceived quality and effectiveness of communication."[25] An additional factor is to be a "good listener." Elmer notes how when we are "good listeners" we not only show the speaker our love for them, but the speaker will feel comfortable to divulge more about themselves with us.[26]

Another factor for effectively building cross-cultural relationships is avoiding an ethnocentric attitude. Lustig and Koester write how we are to contemplate how our "emotional reactions" to "sights, sounds, and smells" in other cultures may reveal our own ethnocentric mindset.[27] An additional factor is to self-disclose with hosts. Dodd writes how if one "under-discloses" in a culture that expects "high-disclosure," or one "over-discloses" in a context that values "low-disclosure," then "cultural conflict" ensues.[28] An added factor is developing a mastery of the local culture. Gudykunst and Kim explain "knowledge" and how it relates to knowing the other culture and differences and similarities between them and us.[29] We are to "be mindful" and recognize the other's perspective and not just our own.[30] The final factor is the importance of assimilating into the local culture and learning the host language well.[31]

It must be noted that I did not explicitly ask the interviewees to share stories with me about struggles they had in building cross-cultural relationships, which would have painted a more comprehensive picture of the interviewees' experiences in cross-cultural relationships. All interviewees who described their struggles in building cross-cultural relationships did so without being explicitly asked in the interview. They were asked what main factors contributed to them building closer relationships with hosts,

---

24. Gudykunst and Kim, *Communicating with Strangers*, 339.
25. Gudykunst and Kim, *Communicating with Strangers*, 341.
26. Elmer, *Cross-Cultural Servanthood*, 122.
27. Lustig and Koester, *Among US*, 160.
28. Dodd, *Dynamics of Intercultural Communication*, 190.
29. Gudykunst and Kim, *Communicating with Strangers*, 280–82.
30. Gudykunst and Kim, *Communicating with Strangers*, 283.
31. Gudykunst and Kim, *Communicating with Strangers*, 292; Gudykunst and Hammer, "Strangers and Hosts," 126; Lingenfelter and Mayers, *Ministering Cross-Culturally*, 114; Elmer, *Cross-Cultural Servanthood*, 66, 77–78.

which resulted in the interviewees telling stories about close relationships they had with hosts.

Interviewees noted that their own friendliness, language proficiency, and easygoing personality were some factors that helped them to reduce anxiety in their interaction with hosts. These experiences parallel what Gudykunst and Kim wrote concerning how we experience increased anxiety when we communicate with those of other ethnic groups, and how our communication will become effective if we can minimize anxiety and uncertainty.[32]

One interviewee admitted that after five years in one Southeast Asian country she was critical of that country, disliked it, and wanted to leave. However, after a longer time living there, her perspective has been transformed. She now understands the necessity of not only avoiding criticizing the host culture but also appreciating and respecting it. This is consistent with the findings of Gudykunst and Sudweeks, who write about how damaging ways to cope with anxiety include criticizing the other culture.[33]

One interviewee talked about how his being a good listener aids him in making closer relationships with hosts. This is consistent with findings that being a good listener is necessary for building effective cross-cultural relationships.[34]

One interviewee explained the mutual happiness she experiences being with host friends and how the hosts see her family as one of their "relatives," because of the intimacy of their relationship with them. These findings correspond with Ted Ward's definition of "empathy" as partly involving "emotional connection."[35]

80 percent of those interviewed described sharing their struggles openly with hosts. Other interviewees failed to share their frustrations with hosts. Some interviewees shared only with either other missionaries or their Chinese leaders. Reasons given for not sharing with host believers included being unwilling to show their own weaknesses as well as thinking the hosts would not understand them. One person noted that in the Middle East it was a challenge for her to self-disclose to her hosts as openly as they expected. Experts on cross-cultural relationships describe

---

32. Gudykunst and Kim, *Communicating with Strangers*, 339–41.

33. Gudykunst and Sudweeks, "Applying a Theory," 365.

34. Gudykunst, *Bridging Differences*, 182–86; Dodd, *Dynamics of Intercultural Communication*, 202–3; Elmer, *Cross-Cultural Servanthood*, 122.

35. Cited in Moreau et al., *Effective Intercultural Communication*, 221.

how those who self-disclose with hosts are more likely to build deeper relationships with the hosts.[36]

One interviewee described how she adjusted to the new culture by learning about the similarities and differences between China and that country. She went to a seminar and also researched their culture and history online. Her experience parallels what some of the experts wrote about needing to understand culture-specific knowledge that relates to that culture's characteristics and customs including what makes that culture unique.[37] Another interviewee talked about how when she had questions about the host culture, she asked her close host friend for help. This approach is similar to what Elmer wrote about the importance of learning *from* others—asking them questions about their culture and lives and letting them teach us about their world.[38]

One interviewee talked about wearing a head covering and long dress to blend into the host Muslim culture; she also mentioned that she goes out to the fields with host women to assist them with farming. These lifestyle choices led to the hosts treating her like she is one of them. Another missionary talked about how he is willing to sleep in host friends' dirty homes in the villages, without bathrooms, electricity or Internet, and commented that the hosts accept him because of his willingness to live with them and like them. These research findings are consistent with what multiple scholars wrote concerning the necessity of following customs and habits of hosts in order to build closer relationships.[39]

When the interviewees were asked about cross-cultural adjustment challenges and aspects about the host culture they dislike, eight of the 25 interviewees mentioned their frustration that hosts are always late and fail to arrive when they say they will. Lingenfelter and Mayers wrote in their classic work *Ministering Cross-Culturally* that each culture perceives time differently. Chapter 3 of their book describes how some cultures are punctual and closely follow time while other cultures are less concerned about

36. Gudykunst and Kim, *Communicating with Strangers*, 333; Lustig and Koester, *Intercultural Competence*, 227–45; Dodd, *Dynamics of Intercultural Communication*, 189–90; Elmer, *Cross-Cultural Conflict*, 157.

37. Lustig and Koester, *Among US*, 69–70; Moreau et al., *Effective Intercultural Communication*, 232–33.

38. Elmer, *Cross-Cultural Servanthood*, 98.

39. Gudykunst and Kim, *Communicating with Strangers*, 292; Gudykunst and Sudweeks, "Applying a Theory," 365–66; Lingenfelter and Mayers, *Ministering Cross-Culturally*, 10–11, 114.

time and how this difference in time perceptions can cause stress when going to a new culture.[40]

Three interviewees talked about how respecting the hosts aided in making tighter relationships with them. These experiences are in agreement with Duane Elmer's comments that we are to treat others with respect, as they are made in God's image.[41]

Nine of the interviewees mentioned how during their first two years on the field a major challenge was related to interpersonal relationships with hosts. One woman described how it was difficult for her in the Middle East to self-disclose with the hosts as much as they expected. Another interviewee in the Middle East became exhausted from her host friends' expectations to spend extensive time with her. Two interviewees in Southeast Asia expressed frustration in often not being able to understand what the hosts were thinking, because of the hosts' indirectness in communication. One interviewee had money stolen by a host Muslim she considered her "best friend." Another interviewee talked about having only shallow relationships with hosts when she first moved onto the field, as her language ability then was not competent enough to communicate at a deep level.

In addition, some of the interviewees described how their friendships with hosts were hindered because of their own deficiencies in the host language. As previously noted, some mentioned having challenges making host friends, for example when interviewees could not understand the spoken language of hosts. Another expressed only being able to befriend hosts who spoke English, because his host language ability was insufficient.

Some of the interviewees talked about other negative interpersonal relationship experiences with hosts. One interviewee noted how a host female student who was studying Chinese became angry with the interviewee when the interviewee refused to help her with her Chinese homework. In another case, there was a misunderstanding regarding what it meant to be a "friend." One interviewee in South Asia noted challenges in befriending local Hindus, because he felt uncomfortable in their homes eating food they had sacrificed to idols.

---

40. Lingenfelter and Mayers, *Ministering Cross-Culturally*, 25–38.
41. Elmer, *Cross-Cultural Servanthood*, 45.

Mission Team as Help or Hindrance?

How mission teams can either help or hinder Chinese missionaries was another theme that emerged from the research. Many missionaries noted a positive experience within their mission agency team. One interviewee articulated her tight relationship with a Chinese teammate in the Middle East, explaining how they mutually encourage and pray for each other. Similarly, three others noted that their strong team has kept them on the field. One interviewee talked about how his teammates have become close friends, and they can share with one another, support each other, and carry one another's burdens. These research findings are consistent with Detlef Blocher's statements that a close relationship with teammates is one of the primary aspects that keeps NSC missionaries on the field.[42] Rob Hay confirms that, since NSCs are very relational, their positive relationships with teammates are key for them staying on the field and lead to greater effectiveness.[43]

Conversely, one interviewee, even within an all-Chinese team, articulated that she failed to get along well with her teammate and this exhausted her. Her experience coincides with Rob Hay's observation that, as important as having a strong team is for retention of NSC missionaries, team conflict can be a weighty distraction for these missionaries.[44] Some Chinese missionaries had struggles within international mission agency teams. One interviewee expressed how hard it was for missionaries coming from a monocultural background like China to thrive when having numerous cultures within their international team. Another similarly noted that, even on a team with other Chinese speakers from Hong Kong, Taiwan, and Singapore, they had conflict in trying to minister together as they all had varying ideas about their lives and ministry. Another interviewee explained the difficulties in working under a Korean team leader, saying that it took her multiple years to learn to work well under him. These interviewees' challenges correspond with Rob Hay's conclusion that team conflict within international teams can be a challenge because people struggle to work well with people who are dissimilar.[45]

---

42. Blocher, "ReMAP I," 15.
43. Hay, "Personal Care—Team Building and Functioning," 163.
44. Hay, "Personal Care—Conflict and Teams," 175.
45. Hay, "Personal Care—Conflict and Teams," 176.

Two interviewees discussed being without a team of people who lived in the same place and with whom they could regularly communicate. Both of these interviewees were independent missionaries without regular contact with teammates, a mission agency, or a home church in China, but who learned the host language well and adjusted well on the field. They did not seem to feel discontented in being without a team.

As for how to prepare Chinese missionaries for serving within an international or Chinese mission agency team on the mission field, one interviewee noted how she wished that her pre-field preparation had included ministering together with people of other countries where she could experience firsthand ministering within a multicultural team. In order to develop positive teamwork during training, another interviewee mentioned the helpfulness of doing everything together as a team for the duration of her training time, which resulted in her working well within a team when moving on the field.

Level of Supportiveness of Mission Agencies

Another emerging theme from the research is the various types and amount of support missionaries received from their mission agency. Twelve of the 25 interviewees were sent through international mission agencies. Many Chinese missionaries described the strong on-field support they had received from such agencies. One interviewee talked about how she had regular contact with her agency's on-field leaders, who provided help and encouragement for her. One interviewee's mission agency provided noteworthy support, and he commented that his agency even provided him a work platform at their language school. Another mentioned how her mission agency leaders encouraged her by avoiding simply giving her instructions, but instead taught her how to think and process her surroundings and relationships on her own. A negative experience regarding on-field support within international mission agencies, though, was one interviewee's report that his mission agency leaders had never lived on the mission field and thus were unable to aid him substantially with ministry guidance in many areas. These experiences parallel Rob Hay's statement that for mission agencies sending NSC missionaries, it is critical to provide practical on-field support.[46]

---

46. Hay, "Personal Care: What it Means," 151.

Eleven of the 25 interviewees were sent through Chinese mission agencies, while two do not belong to mission agencies and were sent independently through house churches in China. Regarding those within Chinese mission agencies, four said that their Chinese agency aided them in managing their finances, providing prayer and member care support, and locating a house church in China to financially support them. Others talked about receiving spiritual support and teaching from their Chinese agency; some mentioned that their mission agency leaders provide weekly teachings online for all of the agency's missionaries. As for negative experiences within Chinese mission agencies, multiple interviewees noted their mission agency leaders' lack of mission experience and thus lack of understanding of life on the field. Therefore, they felt that agency leaders could not provide wise counsel for their ministry. Another interviewee also explained that there was no experienced person on the field to help them with the ministry. The literature failed to mention the importance of having NSC mission agency leaders who have cross-cultural mission experience.

Unique Challenges for Single Missionaries

An additional emerging theme was the unique challenges for single missionaries. Of the 25 missionaries interviewed, eight of them are single female missionaries and two are single male missionaries. Some of these Chinese missionaries seemed to be discontented about still being single. One interviewee, a single male missionary, expressed how his principal problem is that he wants to be married but is still single. One single woman mentioned that it angers her when hosts ask her if she is married. She has the impression that the hosts may be judging her as being strange. Research findings are consistent with Sarah Hay's statement that missionaries must be content about their marital status, whether married or single.[47]

Some single Chinese missionaries within international mission agencies related that having a mentor aided them on the field. One interviewee, who is now married but spent the entirety of her time on the field unmarried, talked about a woman from her agency that she talked to twice per month on video. This woman, who also has served long-term as a missionary, has been a noteworthy encouragement for her. Another interviewee described monthly conversations with her mentors, and how her mentors gave her beneficial suggestions. One female interviewee expressed how her

47. Hay, "Selection: What it Means," 73.

psychological counselors with extensive mission experience aided her in evaluating and understanding her thoughts and emotions, thus giving her valuable guidance and help. One interviewee noted how a mentor from her mission agency had assisted her in resolving team conflict and finding reconciliation. Concerning what type of support they wish they had received but did not, one single female missionary talked about how she wishes she had a mentor to assist her with practical help, guidance or counseling, but this was unavailable to her. Some single missionaries within Chinese mission agencies also noted the lack of having a mentor. The two single males interviewed mentioned how a personal need was to have a mentor to care for them, as they often feel lonely. These missionaries' experiences parallel Peter's wife's suggestion that one way to support single missionaries is to provide a mentor for them who will care for them and for their various needs.[48] Married missionaries interviewed, in contrast, did not mention the importance of having a mentor from their agency help them.

One single missionary woman articulated feeling unsafe and being fearful of going outside late at night. Her experience is in agreement with Peter's wife's comment that single missionary women often feel afraid about their own personal safety.[49]

Challenges of Overcoming Hosts' Stereotypes and Prejudices of Chinese

Another theme arising is the challenge of overcoming host stereotypes and prejudices against Chinese people. One interviewee described how when arriving in Southeast Asia some hosts thought they should be wealthy, like the other Chinese they saw there, and they were unwilling to be their friends when they realized they were poor. However, through spending time with him, the hosts discovered that their previous misconceptions about him were inaccurate and they thus could develop a close friendship with him. Another interviewee talked about how, because of the poor relationship between China and that country, people in the South Asian country he lives in initially may feel tense when they hear he is Chinese. However, they could later trust him and build friendships with him when they saw how proficiently he could speak the host language. These missionaries' experiences

---

48. Peter's Wife, "Challenges of Single Women," 175.
49. Peter's Wife, "Challenges of Single Women," 175.

are consistent with Elmer's recommendation that through learning *from* others we can eliminate mutual stereotypes.[50]

Some interviewees talked about the negative treatment they received from hosts because of prejudice. One interviewee spoke about his experience of prejudice towards Chinese. M-3-4 said, "Host believers and nonbelievers give special treatment to people from America, Europe, and Japan, places that are most developed. I think people should be seen as equals." Two interviewees mentioned how they dislike the host police because the host police think all Chinese are rich since there are many Chinese businessmen there. They related that the police often try to take advantage of the Chinese and cheat them for money. These interviewees talked about how police will treat only Chinese in this way, not Koreans or Americans.

Short-term Missions as Helpful Missionary Preparation

A final emerging theme is that of the benefit of pre-field short-term mission experience for Chinese missionaries. When the interviewees were asked the question of what pre-field preparation was advantageous, six interviewees responded that short-term missions had been beneficial for them. These short-term mission trips were valuable because they helped the interviewees to experience cross-cultural living, develop adaptability, and learn how to practically think deeply about their environment and experiences. Some of the interviewees had an easier adjustment on the mission field, partly as a result of prior short-term mission trips to that country. One interviewee wished he had taken a previous short-term trip to the Middle East before moving there. He felt that such a trip would have increased his understanding of how hard it is to find jobs in the Middle East, and thus would have led him to receive vocational training in China before leaving. Because most Han have relatively limited exposure to people of other ethnicities, as many people mentioned, their short-term mission experience was very good for them to experience another culture and be exposed to other people. Given the specific Chinese situation, the interviews indicate that short-term mission experience can be a valuable preparation increasing cultural awareness of potential Chinese missionaries.

These interviewees' experiences are consistent with what William Taylor and Steve Hoke wrote about the benefit of living cross-culturally in

---

50. Elmer, *Cross-Cultural Servanthood*, 98.

order to prepare missionaries for cross-cultural life on the mission field.[51] Such cross-cultural experience could come through a short-term mission trip. Evelyn Hibbert agrees with the importance of living cross-culturally for an ample amount of time before moving on the mission field, in order to minimize personal ethnocentric tendencies.[52] David Lee writes that the training of Asian missionaries from a monocultural context should involve experiencing crossing cultures and that such experiences can help in developing personal character, cross-cultural ministry skills, and missiological understanding.[53]

Summary

The first research question addressed the ability of Chinese missionaries to build cross-cultural relationships with the hosts and adapt to the host culture. In summary, many of the interviewees thrived in building cross-cultural relationships, learning the host language well, self-disclosing struggles to hosts, and being respected and trusted by hosts. Some interviewees, however, struggled in building cross-cultural relationships, failed to learn the host language well, and did not build trust with hosts or have deep relationships with them. The data confirms that those who succeeded in learning the language, self-disclosing, and building mutually trusting relationships with hosts adjusted better on the field. On the other hand, those who did not do well in these three areas had a harder time adjusting on the field.

The second research question explored how pre-field preparation and on-field support contributed to Chinese missionaries remaining on the mission field. The large majority of the interviewees (23 of 25) received mission training of at least three months. Almost half of the interviewees (12 of 25) lacked a bachelor's degree, but this less formal school education had no perceived negative effect on their effectiveness in learning the language and building cross-cultural relationships. When asked what pre-field preparation the interviewees wish they had received but did not, the most prevalent response (11 of 25) was technical or business training. Similar to struggles of majority world missionaries in general, many of the interviewees reported that a significant challenge was insufficient financial support from churches

---

51. Hoke and Taylor, "Exposure to Other Cultures," 107.
52. Hibbert, *Training Missionaries*, 69.
53. Lee, "Training Cross-Cultural Missionaries," 113.

in China. In addition, a common theme for the interviewees was the prevalence of family blessings contributing to their staying on the field. Also of relevance is the fact that, since this research is qualitative in nature, its findings cannot be generalized to other groups or populations.

Overall, there are many similarities between Chinese missionaries and missionaries sent from other countries. Chinese missionaries have many of the same cross-cultural adjustment and host language learning challenges as missionaries from other countries. These findings were not unexpected; they tend to be consistent with the broader literature in most respects. Chinese missionaries are, in most aspects, like other missionaries. However, given the extreme circumstances from which they come (China), the more difficult contexts in which they work (e.g. Muslim world, Southeast Asia), and very difficult languages that they must learn, they may experience some of the common missionary challenges to a greater degree.

Comparing the Chinese mission movement with other researched majority world mission movements (Korea, Latin America, India, Africa), the Chinese movement is similar in some regards to the Korean movement; they are both from East Asia and have in common the importance of filial piety and the family's support for the missionaries. Another similarity to Korean missionaries is the challenge of ministering cross-culturally when coming from a monocultural context (more than 90 percent of the same ethnicity). A major difference between the Korean mission movement and the Chinese mission movement, however, is that Korea is an economically developed country, while China is developing. Chinese missionaries' struggles with shortages of financial support are more similar to majority world missionaries sent from Latin America, India, and Africa.

Also of note is that the Chinese mission movement comes from a country (China) that has a closed and controlling government, whereas Korea, India, and many countries in Africa and Latin America are countries where Christianity is not controlled and mission agencies are legal. An additional characteristic of the Chinese mission movement is that, based on conversations I have had with reputable sources, many of the missionaries sent out from China are sent from largely rural and poor house church networks and have not received formal school education beyond middle or high school. However, it was not determined if the subjects of this research were from a rural or urban context.

When analyzing the data, factors that emerged as most important to keeping the interviewees on the mission field rather than prematurely returning home include:

- 11 of 25: God's personal calling of them to missions
- 11 of 25: a concern for the spiritual needs of people in the host culture
- 10 of 25: mission agency's support
- 7 of 25: teammates' support
- 7 of 25: home church's support
- 7 of 25: their parents' or other family members' support
- 4 of 25: mentors' support and guidance

Implications

The Relationship of Formal Education and Cross-Cultural Effectiveness

A characteristic of the interviewees was that 11 of the 25 interviewees did not receive formal school education beyond middle or high school. Although these missionaries have a low level of formal school education, they may have received extensive theological education or mission training. Have my findings from this research of Chinese missionaries supported the idea that those with more formal education have a smoother cross-cultural adjustment on the mission field? If anything, at least based on the limited sample of Chinese missionaries I interviewed, the majority of these less educated Chinese missionaries interviewed have paralleled what was written in the ReMAP II book; they are similar to the missionaries from Nigeria who lacked formal education but were still effective in cross-cultural missions.[54]

Many of both the more educated and less educated interviewees seemed to flourish cross-culturally in learning well the host language and effectively making close relationships with hosts. In addition, both the less educated and the college-educated interviewees faced similar challenges on the field. For example, both the more educated and less educated interviewees struggled with the challenge of having a legitimate platform, job,

---

54. Abimbola, "Is Higher Education Required," 62.

and adequate salary on the mission field in order to be self-supporting. Concerning the relationship of mission agency and formal school educational background, nine of the thirteen interviewees who have at least a bachelor's degree belong to international mission agencies. Seven of the eight interviewees without education higher than a middle school degree belong to Chinese mission agencies. There is no clear difference in language ability, retention, or cross-cultural flourishing between those with a bachelor's degree and those without.

The Need to Assist Missionaries in Fulfilling Filial Obligations

One observation of note pertains to the reality of how filial piety in China affects the Chinese mission movement and potential Chinese missionaries. Hung writes how Chinese Christians are deterred from moving to the mission field because of an obligation to fulfill their duty to take care of their aging parents.[55]

Hung suggests that the problem of potential Chinese missionaries being prevented from going to the mission field because of their sense of obligation to their family could be solved by Chinese house churches assisting in taking care of missionaries' parents.[56] M-9-10 mentioned his frustrations that his mission agency failed to let him return every year to see his family. He said, "Chinese people are concerned about family. It is hard that we cannot return to China every year to see our father and mother. If your parents are old and in bad health, and we are both only children, this is stressful for those of us ministering outside China. We have seen many who have left the field because of these pressures." At the end of his comments, M-9-10 added, "And our home church does not care for our parents." Thus, M-9-10's challenges and stress are amplified because his home church in China has not taken the responsibility to take care of his aging parents, which is, according to Hung, what would be ideal. If his home church could carry part of the load in taking care of M-9-10's parents, M-9-10 could minister on the field without feeling guilty for leaving his parents alone in China.

Similar to M-9-10's circumstances were the challenges of F-13-7, who described the pressure she felt after her father passed away. When she was considering moving to Southeast Asia, the chief influence holding her back

---

55. Hung, "Filial Piety and Missionary Calling," 78.
56. Hung, "Filial Piety and Missionary Calling," 78.

was her concern for who would take care of her mother, who was old and in poor health. F-13-7 talked about the importance of parents to children in Chinese culture and discussed how Chinese women who leave behind their parents feel they have failed in fulfilling their filial piety. This was a deterrent for F-13-7 moving onto the field, as she desired to avoid disappointing her family. Nevertheless, the reason she could have peace of mind to move to the mission field was that her sister told F-13-7 that she would adequately take care of their mother. This is what allowed F-13-7 to move to the field without having a guilty conscience.

For Chinese missionaries, it is paramount that someone back in China is helping take care of the aging parents they are leaving behind. M-9-10's lack of care for his aging parents in China has added to his pressure on the mission field; however, on the other side, F-13-7 is able to live on the mission field without guilt because she has someone to take care of her elderly mother—her sister. As Hung wrote, in a country like China with such a substantial emphasis on filial piety, it is essential that someone back in China can aid in taking care of missionaries' aging parents or other family members. This frees up Chinese missionaries, who may otherwise feel guilty for leaving behind their parents, to serve freely on the mission field without such large ongoing distractions. Since filial piety is also a social obligation, failure to fulfill this obligation would also be a poor testimony to Christianity. Hung described the necessity of home churches in China helping to take care of missionaries' elderly parents. For Chinese missionaries, it is supreme that someone back in China is actively assisting in taking care of their aging parents. This caretaker could be another family member or sibling. Alternatively, this caretaker could be someone from the missionary's home church, especially if that missionary's family lacks someone who will carry a heavy part of the load in taking care of the parents.

Providing Adequate Financial Support through Job Skill Training

It would be advantageous for Chinese mission agencies or international mission agencies sending out Chinese missionaries to make some adjustments in their missionary preparation. The most obvious adjustment that mission agencies sending Chinese missionaries need to make in training pertains to better preparing Chinese missionaries to obtain employment and adequate financial support on the field. This could happen by agencies recommending that candidates receive vocational training in specific areas prior to departure for the field. The mission agency could obtain information on what the specific job opportunities for Chinese are in specific locations of ministry. The agency could recommend that their candidates receive the appropriate vocational training that would be suited to that location. M-12-12 is the only interviewee who identified as having received such training, and he talked about how beneficial this training was for his life on the field. On the question of training they wish they had received but did not, 11 of the 25 interviewees mentioned vocational training. They added that such training could prepare them for finding a job, having a stable income, obtaining a steady visa, opening up ministry opportunities, and providing a legitimate identity on the mission field. A stable income, one product of having a job on the field, would result in these missionaries being able to earn money on their own and thus needing to rely less on often unsteady financial support from house churches in China.

Many of the interviewees talked about how their only previous work experience in China was working in house churches. Many of them lacked business or other work experience in China. Thus, particularly without receiving any pre-field skill training before leaving, they move to the mission field with certain limitations. They can learn language full-time for two or three years on a student visa, but problems arise when they desire to stay for a longer time on the mission field. They cannot remain on a student visa long-term. It is not practical or desirable for their whole family to leave their country of service every few months in order to renew a tourist visa. They need real jobs on the field that not only provide them with a visa but also provide them with income and a legitimate position in the society. Ideally, this job on the field would not be a business platform opened purely for the sake of acquiring a visa yet lacking doing much real work (like M-10-8).

These missionaries would benefit from being equipped to obtain legitimate employment on the mission field. Some of the interviewees teach Chinese part-time or full-time and obtain a work visa in this way. For Chinese serving in countries closer to China (e.g. Kazakhstan, Thailand), there is a higher demand to learn Chinese, and educated Chinese could have open doors to teach Chinese there. However, for countries further away from China, such as the Middle East or Africa, there is less demand for learning Chinese and thus jobs teaching Chinese would be scarce. It would be helpful to have multiple job possibilities for Chinese missionaries.

To equip Chinese missionaries for earning an income and obtaining a visa on the field, what type of skills or business training will actually be effective? M-12-12, even with his pre-field vocational training, still has had difficulty operating a profitable business in Central Asia. Ideally, it would be valuable for the trainees to learn about the specific job situation of the country to which they will be moving. Before arriving on the field, they should determine what kinds of jobs are available and in high demand in that country. If a high demand for Chinese teachers exists, then the trainees, especially if they are college educated, can prepare for this before going on the field. They can receive training on teaching Chinese to foreigners and obtain a teaching Chinese certification.

If the trainees have particular professional backgrounds (e.g. engineering, doctor, businessman or woman), they could potentially find jobs in these professions in the foreign country to qualify for a work visa on the field. This could be similar to what is often referred to as "Business as Mission" (BAM). Well-educated Chinese with entrepreneurial business skills could potentially open profitable businesses on the field. Then they could do ministry through those jobs. Less educated Chinese may have fewer opportunities to be professionals or teach Chinese in the host country. Again, the host context needs to be understood before the missionaries move on the field. For Chinese missionaries without previous business experience, however, extended training before they leave for the field would be advised. This could include: learning how to start a sustainable business and make a profit; determining what jobs are most plausible for the country they are moving to; determining which of those jobs they are qualified for based on their personal experiences; and obtaining skill training and appropriate certifications (e.g. chef; Chinese or English teacher; barber).

In seeking work opportunities in the foreign land, it is paramount to avoid having the challenges of M-5-15, who has only a middle school education and no additional training. When he first moved on the mission field, he was without financial support from China and thus had to work full-time in a factory to stay there. Since he worked such hard and long hours in his factory job, he lacked time or energy to learn the host language or make host friends. This situation is problematic, but for less educated Chinese missionaries with no special training, such jobs may be the only ones available. This is why it is so important for less educated missionaries to be properly prepared to start a profit-making business or store.

Ideally, Chinese missionaries can have jobs or start profitable businesses, rather than losing considerable money through starting businesses on the field that just lose money. This can keep them from needing to continue to rely on financial support from churches in China.

9 of the 25 interviewees mentioned that financial support provided by their sending church or agency was inadequate or undependable. This financial stress reveals an even greater need for the mission agencies to develop ways for their Chinese missionaries to receive vocational training before going to the mission field. They need to be prepared to find a job on the field, earn an income, and provide for themselves financially. Another option is for sending churches to support their missionaries at more realistic levels. However, this may not help the missionaries obtain a visa in the same way that job skills or starting a business might.

The Importance of Pre-field Cross-cultural Preparation

Chinese missionaries need two types of pre-field cross-cultural preparation. The first type concerns general cross-cultural adjustment and living skills. This may come through taking short-term mission trips, as was the case for many of the interviewees, and as was suggested by William D. Taylor and Steve Hoke in *Global Mission Handbook*.[57] Jonathan Ingleby suggests experiential cross-cultural mission practice, by living in a dissimilar culture for an extended time and experiencing longer-term challenges with various cross-cultural adjustments (food, language, interpersonal relationships with hosts, time perceptions, team conflict).[58] It is suggested to do this not merely for a few weeks, but at least several months if possible. It is also recommended to simulate life on the field, which would include being in a team environment that requires working together to achieve common tasks for survival and outreach.

The second type of cross-cultural preparation needed is learning about the more specific challenges that Chinese missionaries might face. An adjustment in Chinese missionary training would be to teach them the most predominant cross-cultural adjustment difficulties for Chinese missionaries. Such preparation could be country specific. This way, Chinese missionaries can understand common challenges that others have already faced, and be able to minimize their own culture shock when they arrive on the field.

The most common cross-cultural challenges faced were:

57. Hoke and Taylor, "Exposure to Other Cultures," 107.
58. Ingleby, "Preparation Time," 108.

- 11 of 25: difficulty adjusting to food and diet
- 10 of 25: difficulty learning the language
- 9 of 25: difficulty with interpersonal relationships with hosts
- 6 of 25: difficulty with adjusting to the hosts' perception of time
- 6 of 25: difficulty with team conflict

A resource that could be used for training in these areas is Lingenfelter and Mayers' *Ministering Cross-Culturally*. It would be beneficial for trainees to learn about various countries' differences in values related to time, judgment, handling crisis, goals, self-worth, and vulnerability.[59] Doing this can aid future Chinese missionaries in better understanding some cultural differences between various countries, and thus help them have a smoother cross-cultural adjustment process when moving onto the mission field. In addition to William D. Taylor and Steve Hoke's edited work *Global Mission Handbook* (2009), other beneficial resources for training Chinese missionaries for cross-cultural ministry include: *Training Missionaries: Principles and Possibilities*, by Evelyn Hibbert (2016); "Training Cross-Cultural Missionaries from the Asian Context," written by David Tai-Woong Lee (2008); and, *Integral Ministry Training: Design and Evaluation*, edited by Robert Brynjolfson and Jonathan Lewis (2014).

Also of benefit would be mission agencies preparing Chinese missionaries for other common cross-cultural challenges that previous Chinese missionaries have faced in adjusting to the host people or culture. For example, six people responded that the hosts have different values relating to honesty. Other common responses concerning challenges were: how the host men treat them as women (three people); police corruption in the foreign country (three people); hosts' indirectness in communication (two people); and, how the hosts view financial matters, such as lending and borrowing (two people).

Partnership between International Mission Agencies and Chinese Mission Agencies

Comparisons can be made and implications drawn by comparing the experience of those interviewees belonging to international mission agencies and those belonging to Chinese mission agencies. As previously mentioned,

---

59. Lingenfelter and Mayers, *Ministering Cross-Culturally*, 19.

most of those with a bachelor's degree belonged to international mission agencies, while those who received no formal school education beyond middle or high school usually belonged to Chinese mission agencies. Some Chinese missionaries may prefer to join a Chinese mission agency where Chinese is the language of communication. For those missionaries belonging to international mission agencies, English would usually be the primary language used within the team and agency. Both those belonging to international agencies and Chinese agencies generally belonged to a team. Many within both kinds of agencies had positive team experiences. Though team conflict was mentioned more for those within international agencies, team conflict also existed for some within Chinese agencies. The eight single women that all belonged to international agencies generally received much greater support from their agencies compared to the two single men within Chinese agencies. Both those belonging to international agencies and those within Chinese agencies had challenges of irregular and insufficient finances. Interviewees belonging to both kinds of agencies had difficulties finding a job or starting a business platform on the field.

A large difference in the experiences of those belonging to international agencies compared to those within Chinese agencies is that most of those within international agencies had a mentor and someone with mission experience who could give ministry and other guidance to the missionaries. On the other hand, those belonging to Chinese agencies generally lacked having a mentor or leader with mission experience who could mentor or guide them. Most of the ten interviewees who mentioned being deficient in having an experienced mentor or leader belonged to Chinese agencies.

Most of the international agencies have experienced personnel and overall stronger infrastructure. These findings indicate that a form of partnership between the international agencies and Chinese agencies could be beneficial. The international agencies could help in providing mentors or missionary care for Chinese missionaries within Chinese mission agencies. As the Chinese mission agencies have been in existence for a relatively short time compared to most international agencies, Chinese agencies lack the structures that have been developed within international agencies. International agencies can not only help Chinese agencies by providing support such as member care or mentorship, but the international agencies can give guidance to the Chinese agency leaders in forming their own similar member care or other structures within their own agencies.

Discovering Creative Ways to Work Under Security Constraints and Risks

A difference between the Chinese mission movement and most other majority world mission movements is that Chinese missionaries are sent from an oppressive political setting in which Christianity is strictly controlled. All of these Chinese missionaries are sent from house churches in China, which are technically illegal, and are becoming increasingly persecuted by the central government. In countries with religious freedom, unlike in China, it is possible to have open mission conferences and mission organizations. It is possible to conduct research in detail and with precision. However, this openness in missions is not a possibility for the Chinese mission movement. Open mission conferences or organizations cannot exist within China. Mission agency leaders cannot collaborate openly with one another. Any research or writing about the Chinese mission movement is anecdotal and imprecise.

David Ro claims that China has the largest up-and-coming mission movement arising from a country with an oppressive political regime in which Christianity is strictly controlled.[60] A repeated theme for the Chinese missionaries interviewed was how China's sensitive security affects them. I have heard through reputable sources of instances when the Chinese government has heavily interrogated Chinese missionaries when they are visiting China, though these cases remain the minority. However, the increased persecution and surveillance of Chinese house churches in China by the Chinese government over the last year has had its effects on the Chinese mission movement, as is shown below.

F-6-4 talked about how her support from China may be cut off because of the closing of house churches in Northwest China. She said, "Now we are supported by a church in China, but now difficulties exist with house churches in China, and in my home province in Northwest China it is harder for my house church to meet now. Sometimes our financial support cuts off. Because of their situation, they cannot fully support us. Now we need a new job here, so as to support ourselves."

F-6-6 and M-5-15 explained that, because of the sensitive environment in China for Christians now, they must be careful in their correspondence with Christians in China. F-6-6 said, "They have a sister at my home church who regularly communicates with me. I share with her. Then she will write

---

60. Ro as cited in Zylstra, "Made in China," 21.

these matters and tell others. [This is how we do it now], because now it is unsafe to send such letters or emails." M-5-15 said, "We used to regularly interact with our supporting church more than we do now. Previously we wrote them a prayer letter each month. Now because of security issues in China, I told the pastor that unless we have an emergency, we would not contact them. This is for their security and for ours."

So, whether the interviewees explicitly mentioned it or not, the Chinese government's recent increased restrictions on house churches and on missionaries has had an impact on them. For some, this increased surveillance means that it is harder for house churches in China supporting them to regularly send them money. Another potential problem is that of supporting house churches in China being broken into smaller groups by the police. If this occurs, suddenly the house church congregants are split up, making it harder for them to continue regular financial donations to the church or their missionaries. Another way Chinese house church pressures impact Chinese missionaries could be in the form of having less contact with a representative from the church, as was the case with M-5-15. Also, there could be increased psychological stress for Chinese missionaries each time they return to China. They may worry whether or not the Chinese government will arrest or interrogate them, or confiscate their passports and inhibit them from returning to the mission field. The increasing persecution of house churches in China by the government is an additional reason why Chinese missionaries need to be prepared and equipped to financially support themselves on the mission field, so as to be financially independent of house churches in China.

Other Factors that Contributed to Chinese Missionary Retention

Analyzing other factors that contribute to Chinese missionary retention, support from within their agency was a factor that was commonly noted as contributing to keeping the interviewed missionaries on the field. Six noted comprehensive support from their international agency. Others expressed how international agencies assisted primarily with finances and other needs, rather than with guidance in ministry. As for those within Chinese mission agencies, four said they receive comprehensive support from their agency. Others mentioned spiritual support and teaching they receive from their Chinese agency, although some had negative experiences with their Chinese mission agency. There were two cases of relatively independent missionaries who seemed to not be considerably hindered in their ministry by their independence, and some interviewees had negative experiences within their international or Chinese mission agency. Nevertheless, it is recommended that those involved with Chinese missionary sending urge potential missionaries to join a mission agency. Ideally, mission agencies can provide significant support for these missionaries, thus aiding in their retention.

A positive aspect of joining a mission agency is being a part of a team. Seven interviewees commented on how teammates' support helps keep them on the field. Although there were some interviewees who mentioned the stress of experiencing team conflict on the field, it is still suggested that mission agencies sending Chinese missionaries place their missionaries within teams, ideally ministering together within the same city and regularly seeing one another. In doing so, these missionaries can encourage and support one another, contributing to mutual increased retention and effectiveness in learning the host language and building deep relationships with hosts on the field.

Many interviewees also noted the significance of mission agencies providing a mentor experienced in missions who can provide member care and on-field guidance. Four interviewees noted how having a mentor contributed to the interviewees' retention. On the other hand, regarding on-field support the interviewees wish they had received but have not, ten missionaries express the desire for someone experienced in missions in their agency to guide them or someone to give them missionary care. In addition, for most of the ten single missionaries interviewed, having a mentor with whom they could regularly communicate was critical for their retention. Many missionaries sent through Chinese mission agencies noted that they lack leaders within their agency who were experienced in missions and could provide them with practical on-field support and guidance. In addition, F-8-10 expressed that international agencies do not always know how to care for Chinese missionaries. Thus it is recommended that mission agencies sending Chinese missionaries strive hard to have mentors or leaders who are experienced in missions and who can provide missionary care and guidance for both single and married Chinese missionaries.

An additional factor in Chinese missionary retention is support from churches in China. Ten interviewees talked about the support they received from churches in China. Seven of these received comprehensive support from their home church, which contributed to their well-being. Others mentioned how their mission agency introduced them to a church in China that would "adopt" them, providing them with both financial and prayer support. Whether through support from the missionary's home church or another church in China introduced by the mission agency, it is important that each Chinese missionary receives consistent spiritual, prayer, and—if needed—financial support from house churches in China. Such support from churches in China should not just be for the missionary's initial years on the field, but ongoing. Having this steady support not only aids in the missionaries' retention, but the churches in China can also be spiritually edified through their ongoing support of and relationship with these missionaries.

Analyzing other factors in Chinese missionary retention, eleven interviewees mentioned the importance of God's personal calling. Thus, mission agencies should be encouraged to discuss Chinese missionary candidates' calling to missions during the candidacy process. This factor was also mentioned in the original ReMAP study. Lack of a calling was considered a major factor in avoidable attrition.[61] In addition, eleven interviewees noted how a concern for the spiritual needs of people in the host culture was a noteworthy contributing factor for keeping them on the field. Since this is quite important, mission agencies can emphasize the spiritual needs of the host culture both in recruiting new missionaries and in finding house churches to financially support missionaries.

---

61. Brierley, "Missionary Attrition," 94.

6

Conclusion and Recommendations

THIS CHAPTER WILL COVER the key conclusions from the study. Additionally, it will make recommendations for further research. This study began by looking at relevant research questions. The first research question addressed how Chinese cross-cultural workers have succeeded or struggled in cross-cultural relationships. The second research question analyzed what pre-field and on the field experiences have contributed to Chinese cross-cultural workers' retention in cross-cultural service.

There are four key conclusions that come out of this study. First, the data and analysis reveal that finances are a significant challenge for Chinese missionaries. Many of these missionaries receive some financial support from house churches in China. However, this financial support is often insufficient to meet the needs of the missionaries on the field. These findings are not surprising, as China is a developing nation, which means that Chinese house churches have less money to contribute to Chinese missionaries. This means that many of the interviewees receive unsteady and inconsistent financial support from China. This is an added stress for the Chinese missionaries. An additional factor regarding finances for Chinese missionaries is that the Chinese government's recent increase in persecution of house churches in China has financially affected Chinese missionaries. Missionaries may have financial support from China cut off if police in China try to close down house churches that support them. This issue of shortage of finances is an issue related to missionary retention, as some Chinese missionaries may need to permanently leave the mission field as a result of not having adequate financial support.

The second key conclusion from the study was the need for pre-field vocational training. As mentioned above, Chinese missionaries struggle with a lack of sufficient funds to live on the mission field. Nearly half of the 25 interviewees mentioned that they wished they had received pre-field preparation in the area of vocational training. The missionaries interviewed have had difficulties earning an income on the mission field, which has been a challenge not only for those missionaries with less formal school education but also for those with more formal school education. If these missionaries could earn income on the field, they could rely less on the tenuous financial support from churches in China. In addition, vocational training would help the Chinese missionaries to not only earn an income on the field, but also obtain a long-term work visa, maintain a legitimate position in the host society, and have avenues to build relationships with hosts for the purpose of ministry.

The third key conclusion is the impact of filial piety on Chinese missionaries. Seven of the 25 interviewees noted how their family's support is one of the main factors for them remaining on the mission field. However, one of the interviewees mentioned how difficult it has been for her that her family does not support her to be on the mission field. For Chinese missionaries, their family's support is critical. This finding is not surprising, as the Chinese society is one in which filial piety is central. In China, everyone is expected to respect his or her elders, especially within a family setting. It is not surprising that family elders' support would be a main factor for why Chinese missionaries move onto the field initially and why they remain on the field. This factor of filial piety is related to missionary retention: the receiving of family support contributes to retention while lack of support negatively affects retention.

The fourth key conclusion is that there is no correlation between educational achievement and cross-cultural effectiveness. Contrary to what I expected, the data indicated that those who have received less formal education were not less effective in cross-cultural adjustment and relationship building on the field compared to those with more formal education. In this research, many of those with only a middle school education flourished on the field in building relationships with hosts, learning the host language, and adjusting cross-culturally. In addition, some who had a bachelor's degree seemed to struggle in building cross-cultural relationships and adjusting on the field. Eleven of the 25 interviewees had no more than a middle or high school education. Thirteen of the 25 interviewees had at least a bachelor's degree. But, as previously mentioned, there was no clear correlation between the missionary's formal education background and their cross-cultural adjustment and language learning on the mission field. In addition, the missionaries' formal educational levels seemed to have no positive or negative impact on their retention.

Possibilities abound for future research among Chinese missionaries. One topic would be conducting field research within a Chinese missionary training center, analyzing the dynamics, strengths, and weaknesses of their training. This dissertation was not intended to investigate the specifics of Chinese missionary training but rather sought to present a broad picture of Chinese missionary experience. It would be advantageous to conduct further research, delving into each specific facet of Chinese missionary training and focusing on the effectiveness of Chinese missionary training models, including what could be revised or added. Also helpful would be to examine the different types of ministry that Chinese missionaries are involved in on the mission field, which was not approached in this dissertation. Another potential option would be to do field research investigating how Chinese house churches prepare and support the missionaries they send, including how they raise funding for their missionaries from house churches in their house church network. Also beneficial would be conducting quantitative studies among a larger sample to discover how widespread the factors discovered by my research are for Chinese missionaries. Another relevant study would be research into factors relating to shame and honor. Possible questions could include: Does fear of shame keep Chinese missionaries on the field? How might shame be experienced by missionaries who return early? An additional potential field for research is the experience of Chinese missionaries who belong to international mission agencies.

Anecdotal reports claim that Chinese missionaries have difficulties in cross-cultural relationships and communication with the hosts on the field, and that avoidable attrition rates are high. This research did not test this claim about Chinese missionary attrition, because it only studied missionaries who had persevered and did not return home prematurely. Much like missionaries from other countries, some who remained on the field struggled cross-culturally and have had many cross-cultural relationship challenges. However, the majority of these interviewees seem to have close relationships with hosts, are emphasizing learning or speaking the host language, and have relationships characterized by mutual trust, concern, and love for one another.

This research is the first to empirically research the Chinese mission movement in terms of cross-cultural adjustment and missionary retention. As previously mentioned, the experience of missionaries

CONCLUSION AND RECOMMENDATIONS

interviewed from the Chinese mission movement is consistent with the findings in the literature on missions and on majority world missions. Nevertheless, the Chinese mission movement does have unique aspects related to additional challenges arising from the oppressive government of China as well as how many Chinese missionaries being sent out are without formal school education beyond middle or high school. Some other unique factors for Chinese missionaries are related to filial piety, financial challenges due to inadequate or inconsistent support, and prejudices that Chinese face in other lands.

It is hoped that the findings of this research will better inform those involved in the sending of Chinese missionaries so they can thus provide superior pre-field training and on-field support of such missionaries. Equally important, it is hoped that the findings from this research will benefit mission agency leaders in increasing Chinese missionary effectiveness in cross-cultural adjustment and retention. Leaders in the Chinese mission movement will need to give attention to better preparing Chinese missionaries to obtain employment on the field so they can be less dependent upon financial support from churches in China. In addition, leaders in the Chinese mission movement will need to encourage house churches to assist Chinese missionaries in the area of providing care for the missionaries' aging parents that remain in China.

Appendix A
Interview Protocol

Pre-Interview:

0.1. Background Info:

    0.1.1 Are you married? Do you have children? How old are they? What kind of education do your kids have?

    0.1.2 What country or region of the world do you minister in?

    0.1.3 How long have you been on the mission field?

    0.1.4 From which region in China are you from? (NW, SW, NE, SE, Central)

    0.1.5 What is your highest education level (bachelor's, high school, middle school, etc.)?

    0.1.6 What ethnicity are you? Han Chinese or another?

    0.1.7 Do you belong to an international mission agency, a Chinese mission agency, or are you just sent through a house church?

    0.1.8 What kind of visa do you have there (work, student, etc.)?

    0.1.9 Are you connected to an expat team there?

1. Nearly all cross-cultural missionaries face challenges in adjusting to living in a new culture and country, like when I first moved to China. Tell me about your experience adjusting to living in a new culture. Tell me a story about it.

    1.1 What particular challenges did you face? Can you give an example?

    1.2 Most people experience what is called "culture" shock" during the first year of living in another country: stress, disorientation, homesickness, etc. Did you experience anything like that? If so how did you cope with it?

APPENDIX A: INTERVIEW PROTOCOL

2. What kinds of pre-field preparation for missionary service did you receive? What was helpful?

> 2.1 Did you have pre-field training? If so, can you tell me how long it was and what it consisted of? What was helpful?
>
> 2.2 What preparations do you wish you had had pre-field, but did not?

3. When I first moved to China I had many challenges making relationships with Chinese. Tell me about your relationships with host people. Can you give an example?

> 3.1 Do you have any close relationships with host people? How did that relationship develop?
>
> 3.2 [To those missionaries who have thrived more in cross-cultural relationships]: Is there anything in particular you do to develop deeper relationships with host people? Can you give an example?
>
> 3.3 What do you most appreciate about the host culture and people? Can you give an example?
>
> 3.4 What aspects are most difficult about the host culture and people? Can you give an example?
>
> 3.5 How well do you understand the host culture? Can you give any examples?
>
> 3.6 When you experience frustrations, are there any host people there you can talk to about that? Please explain.

4. When I first moved to China, I realized how difficult it is to learn a foreign language and learn Chinese. Have you attempted to learn the host language? If so, how? If not, why not?

> 4.1 How would you describe your level of proficiency in the host language?
>
> – Can you shop and conduct simple business such as banking?
>
> – Do you feel you can carry on casual conversation?
>
> – Do you read newspapers or other material in the host language?
>
> – Do you feel you are able to teach or preach in the host language?
>
> – With what situations or tasks to you feel that you reach the limits of your language ability?

APPENDIX A: INTERVIEW PROTOCOL

5. Overall, how comfortable do you feel living in that country?

> 5.1 Can you give examples when you have felt comfortable and "at home"?
>
> 5.2. Can you give examples of when you have felt uncomfortable?

6. Many missionaries permanently leave the mission field prior to completion of their anticipated time of service. You are still on the field. Have there been any most significant factors that have helped you stay on the field? Please explain. Any others?

> 6.1 What kinds of support structures (e.g. teammates' support, mission agency leadership, mission field leadership, conferences, other trainings) have helped contribute to your missionary retention? Any others?
>
> 6.2 Has there been any ongoing support on the field that you wish you had had, but have not? Any others?

7. Are there any other positive or negative experiences you or your family have had on the mission field that you want to tell me about? Please explain or give an example. Any others?

Appendix B
Informed Consent Letter

Background and Purpose

OVER THE PAST FEW decades, there have been an increasing number of Chinese missionaries sent across the globe. I am interested to learn about and understand Chinese missionaries' experiences on the mission field. What kinds of common problems or challenges do they have? How are their relationships with hosts? What causes so many Chinese missionaries to leave the mission field within two or three years? What factors might contribute to Chinese missionaries staying long-term on the mission field? I will be interviewing Chinese missionaries from many different mission organizations.

This interview is being conducted as part of doctoral study under the direction of the faculty of Trinity International University (USA). During the interviews on WhatsApp or Skype, I will use an audio recorder on the computer to record the interview. The interview will last approximately 1 hour.

I will be the only person who will have access to personally identifiable information. The information you share with me will be anonymous. No one else will have access to it. Your personal information will be anonymous and not disclosed. Your personal identity will nowhere appear in the written study, and no information that might identify you will be revealed. The project is approved by *Trinity International University*.

It is voluntary for you to participate in this project, and you can withdraw from it at any moment. You do not need to give any reason to me if you withdraw. I will delete any recording done before the withdrawal and not refer to the interview in the project report if you withdraw from the project.

APPENDIX B: INFORMED CONSENT LETTER

If you wish to participate in the project please give verbal affirmation that you have been informed and agree to the conditions of the interview. If you have any questions regarding this research feel free to contact me by phone or email.

Sincerely,
Tabor Laughlin
Trinity International University

Appendix C

Initial Email Correspondence with Missionaries

Hello _____.

Nice to meet you.

I am a PhD student at Trinity Evangelical Divinity School in the U.S. I received your contact information through _____. I am researching Chinese missionaries and their adjustments in foreign cultures. My goal is to help Chinese missionaries be more effective and fruitful. I am looking for Chinese missionaries to interview. If you are willing to help out, the interview would take about one hour. Everything in the interview will remain confidential. The interview will all be in Chinese. I will be interviewing Chinese missionaries from many different mission organizations. Is it true that you are a missionary from Mainland China? Are you living outside of China? Are you ministering to non-Chinese there? Have you been living on the mission field at least two years? Thanks so much for any help you can give me.

Tabor Laughlin

Appendix D

Initial Email Correspondence with Missionary Contacts

Dear _____,

This summer I will begin interviewing Chinese missionaries from Mainland China for my dissertation research at TEDS. I will interview them in Chinese, using Skype. Do you know of any Chinese missionaries who fit the below descriptions?

I am looking for Chinese missionaries who fit all these descriptions:

1. from Mainland China (not Hong Kong, Macau, Taiwan, or Chinese churches outside China)
2. Been on the mission field at least 2 years
3. Serving outside China
4. Ministering to non-Chinese on the mission field
5. Been officially sent out from Mainland China as "missionaries" through international or Chinese mission agencies

Any way you can help me would be appreciated. I am hoping to interview about 30 Chinese missionaries total, representing multiple house church networks and regions of China.

Please contact me if you have any ideas or can introduce me to anyone who fits the above requirements. And pray for me in this research that the Lord may guide me and that it may have some impact on the sending of missionaries from China.

Blessings.
Tabor Laughlin

Bibliography

Abimbola, Nathaniel. "Is Higher Education Required for Effective Mission Work?" In *Worth Keeping: Global Perspectives on Best Practice in Missionary Retention*, edited by Rob Hay, 61–64. Globalization of Mission Series. Pasadena, CA: William Carey Library, 2007.

Adeyemo, Tokunboh. "Profiling a Globalized and Evangelical Missiology." In *Global Missiology for the 21st Century: The Iguassu Dialogue*, edited by William D. Taylor, 259–70. Grand Rapids: Baker, 2000.

Allen, Frank. "Why Do They Leave: Reflections on Attrition." *Evangelical Missions Quarterly* 22.2 (1986) 118–22.

Ang, Henry T. "The Role of the Chinese Church in World Missions." MDiv thesis, Grace Theological Seminary, 1985.

Anyomi, Seth. "African Missionary Movement." In *Missionary Movement of the Non-Western Churches: Compendium of 2010 East-West Mission Forum*, edited by Timothy K. Park and Steve K. Eom, 45–54. Pasadena, CA: East-West Center for Missions Research and Development, 2010.

———. "Attrition in Ghana." In *Too Valuable to Lose: Exploring the Causes and Cures of Missionary Attrition*, edited by William D. Taylor, 161–70. Globalization of Mission Series. Pasadena, CA: William Carey Library, 1997a.

———. "Mission Agency Screening and Orientation and Effect of Attrition Factors: Perspective of the New Sending Countries." In *Too Valuable to Lose: Exploring the Causes and Cures of Missionary Attrition*, edited by William D. Taylor, 229–40. Globalization of Mission Series. Pasadena, CA: William Carey Library, 1997b.

Bernard, H. Russell. *Research Methods in Anthropology: Qualitative and Quantitative Approaches*. Lanham, MD: Altamira Press, 2006.

Blocher, Detlef. "Good Agency Practices: Lessons from ReMAP II." *Evangelical Missions Quarterly* 41 (2005) 228–37.

———. "Member Care: What it Means." In *Worth Keeping: Global Perspectives on Best Practice in Missionary Retention*, edited by Rob Hay, 182–88. Globalization of Mission Series. Pasadena, CA: William Carey Library, 2007.

———. "ReMAP I." In *Worth Keeping: Global Perspectives on Best Practice in Missionary Retention*, edited by Rob Hay, 9–22. Globalization of Mission Series. Pasadena, CA: William Carey Library, 2007.

Blocher, Detlef, and Jonathan Lewis. "Further Findings in the Research Data." In *Too Valuable to Lose: Exploring the Causes and Cures of Missionary Attrition*, edited by William D. Taylor, 105–26. Globalization of Mission Series. Pasadena, CA: William Carey Library, 1997.

BIBLIOGRAPHY

Brant, Howard. "Seven Essentials of Majority World Emerging Mission Movements." In *Missions from the Majority World: Progress, Challenges, and Case Studies*, edited by Enoch Wan and Michael Pocock, 35–58. Pasadena, CA: William Carey Library, 2009.

Brierley, Peter W. "Missionary Attrition: The ReMAP Research Report." In *Too Valuable to Lose: Exploring the Causes and Cures of Missionary Attrition*, edited by William D. Taylor, 85–104. Globalization of Mission Series. Pasadena, CA: William Carey Library, 1997.

Carvalho, Decio de. "Latin American Missionary Movement." In *Missionary Movement of the Non-Western Churches*, edited by Timothy K. Park and Steve K. Eom, 55–68. Pasadena, CA: East-West Center for Missions Research and Development, 2010.

Chan, Wang Kay. "On the Nurturing of Chinese Cross-Cultural Missionaries." DMin diss., Logos Evangelical Seminary, 2012.

Chang, Philip. "Overcoming Low Financial Support by Sending 'Tentmakers' and 'Finishers.'" In *Worth Keeping: Global Perspectives on Best Practice in Missionary Retention*, edited by Rob Hay, 354–57. Globalization of Mission Series. Pasadena, CA: William Carey Library, 2007.

Cho, David J. "A Diagnostic Survey of Missionary Movement in Korea." In *World Mission: Building Bridges or Barriers?: Papers Presented at the Missions Commission Conference of the World Evangelical Fellowship Held at Bad Liebenzell, Germany*, edited by Theodore Williams, 89–93. Bangalore, India: World Evangelical Fellowship, 1979.

CMTC. "Back to Jesus Christ!" https://wenku.baidu.com/view/0424e7b7aef8941ea76e0575.html. 2014.

Deiros, Pablo. "COMIBAM." In *Evangelical Dictionary of World Missions*, edited by A. Scott Moreau, 211–12. Baker Reference Library. Grand Rapids: Baker, 2000.

Dodd, Carley H. *Dynamics of Intercultural Communication*. 5th ed. Boston: McGraw-Hill, 1998.

———. "An Introduction to Intercultural Effectiveness Skills." In *Intercultural Skills for Multicultural Societies*, edited by Carley H. Dodd and Frank F. Montalvo, 3–12. Washington, DC: SIETAR, 1987.

Donovan, Kath, and Ruth Myors. "Reflections on Attrition in Career Missionaries: A Generational Perspective Into the Future." In *Too Valuable to Lose: Exploring the Causes and Cures of Missionary Attrition*, edited by William D. Taylor, 41–74. Globalization of Mission Series. Pasadena, CA: William Carey Library, 1997.

Dooley, Marianna H. "Intercultural Competency in Relation to Missionary Effectiveness: Implications for on-Field Training." PhD diss., Trinity International University, 1998.

Ekstrom, Bertil. "The Selection Process and the Issue of Attrition: Perspective of the New Sending Countries." In *Too Valuable to Lose: Exploring the Causes and Cures of Missionary Attrition*, edited by William D. Taylor, 183–94. Globalization of Mission Series. Pasadena, CA: William Carey Library, 1997.

Elmer, Duane. *Cross-Cultural Conflict: Building Relationships for Effective Ministry*. Downers Grove, IL: InterVarsity, 1993.

———. *Cross Cultural Connections: Stepping out and Fitting in around the World*. Downers Grove, IL: InterVarsity, 2002.

———. *Cross-Cultural Servanthood: Serving the World in Christlike Humility*. Downers Grove, IL: InterVarsity, 2006.

Fulton, Brent. "China: A Tale of Two Churches?" In *China's Reforming Churches: Mission, Polity, and Ministry in the Next Christendom*, edited by Bruce P. Baugus, 177–97. Grand Rapids: Reformation Heritage, 2014.

BIBLIOGRAPHY

―――. *China's Urban Christians: A Light That Cannot Be Hidden*. Eugene, OR: Pickwick Publications, 2015.

Giron, Rodolfo. "An Integrated Model of Missions." In *Too Valuable to Lose: Exploring the Causes and Cures of Missionary Attrition*, edited by William D. Taylor, 25–40. Globalization of Mission Series. Pasadena, CA: William Carey Library, 1997.

Goossaert, Vincent, and David Palmer. *The Religious Question in Modern China*. Chicago: University of Chicago Press, 2011.

Guarneri, Julio. "COMIBAM: Calling Latin Americans to the Global Challenge." In *Missions from the Majority World: Progress, Challenges, and Case Studies*, edited by Enoch Wan and Michael Pocock, 221–62. Pasadena, CA: William Carey Library, 2009.

Gudykunst, William B. "Anxiety/Uncertainty Management (AUM) Theory: Current Status." In *Intercultural Communication Theory*, edited by Richard L. Wiseman, 8–58. International and Intercultural Communication Annual 19. Thousand Oaks, CA: Sage, 1995.

―――. *Bridging Differences: Effective Intergroup Communication*. 4th ed. Thousand Oaks, CA: Sage, 2004.

―――. "Toward a Theory of Effective Interpersonal and Intergroup Communication: An Anxiety/Uncertainty Management (AUM) Perspective." In *Intercultural Communication Competence*, edited by Richard L. Wiseman, and Jolene Koester, 33–71. International and Intercultural Communication Annual 17. Thousand Oaks, CA: Sage, 1993.

―――. "Uncertainty and Anxiety." In *Theories in Intercultural Communication*, edited by William B. Gudykunst and Young Yun Kim, 115–26. Newbury Park, CA: Sage, 1988.

Gudykunst, William B, and Mitchell R. Hammer. "Strangers and Hosts: An Uncertainty Reduction Based Theory of Intercultural Adaptation." In *Cross-Cultural Adaptation: Current Approaches*, edited by Young Yun Kim and William B. Gudykunst, 106–32. Newbury Park, CA: Sage, 1988.

Gudykunst, William B., and Sandra Sudweeks. "Applying a Theory of Intercultural Adaptation." In *Readings on Communicating with Strangers*, edited by William B. Gudykunst and Young Yun Kim, 358–68. New York: McGraw-Hill, 1992.

Gudykunst, William B., and Young Yun Kim. *Communicating with Strangers: An Approach to Intercultural Communication*. 4th ed. Boston: McGraw-Hill, 2003.

Hay, Rob. "Education." In *Worth Keeping: Global Perspectives on Best Practice in Missionary Retention*, edited by Rob Hay, 55. Globalization of Mission Series. Pasadena, CA: William Carey Library, 2007.

―――. "Finances." In *Worth Keeping: Global Perspectives on Best Practice in Missionary Retention*, edited by Rob Hay, 339–40. Globalization of Mission Series. Pasadena, CA: William Carey Library, 2007.

―――. "Home Office." In *Worth Keeping: Global Perspectives on Best Practice in Missionary Retention*, edited by Rob Hay, 361–62. Globalization of Mission Series. Pasadena, CA: William Carey Library, 2007.

―――. "Member Care." In *Worth Keeping: Global Perspectives on Best Practice in Missionary Retention*, edited by Rob Hay, 181–82. Globalization of Mission Series. Pasadena, CA: William Carey Library, 2007.

―――. "Personal Care." In *Worth Keeping: Global Perspectives on Best Practice in Missionary Retention*, edited by Rob Hay, 149–51. Globalization of Mission Series. Pasadena, CA: William Carey Library, 2007.

BIBLIOGRAPHY

———. "Personal Care: What it Means." In *Worth Keeping: Global Perspectives on Best Practice in Missionary Retention*, edited by Rob Hay, 151–53. Globalization of Mission Series. Pasadena, CA: William Carey Library, 2007.

———. "Personal Care—Conflict and Teams." In *Worth Keeping: Global Perspectives on Best Practice in Missionary Retention*, edited by Rob Hay, 175–76. Globalization of Mission Series. Pasadena, CA: William Carey Library, 2007.

———. "Personal Care—Conflict and Teams: What it Means." In *Worth Keeping: Global Perspectives on Best Practice in Missionary Retention*, edited by Rob Hay, 176–77. Globalization of Mission Series. Pasadena, CA: William Carey Library, 2007.

———. "Personal Care—Team Building and Functioning." In *Worth Keeping: Global Perspectives on Best Practice in Missionary Retention*, edited by Rob Hay, 163–64. Globalization of Mission Series. Pasadena, CA: William Carey Library, 2007.

———. "Personal Care—Team Building and Functioning: What it Means." In *Worth Keeping: Global Perspectives on Best Practice in Missionary Retention*, edited by Rob Hay, 164–67. Globalization of Mission Series. Pasadena, CA: William Carey Library, 2007.

———. "Preparation Time." In *Worth Keeping: Global Perspectives on Best Practice in Missionary Retention*, edited by Rob Hay, 105–6. Globalization of Mission Series. Pasadena, CA: William Carey Library, 2007.

———. "Selection—Calling and Tested Call: What it Means." In *Worth Keeping: Global Perspectives on Best Practice in Missionary Retention*, edited by Rob Hay, 94–95. Globalization of Mission Series. Pasadena, CA: William Carey Library, 2007.

Hay, Sarah. "Selection: What it Means." In *Worth Keeping: Global Perspectives on Best Practice in Missionary Retention*, edited by Rob Hay, 71–74. Globalization of Mission Series. Pasadena, CA: William Carey Library, 2007.

Hedlund, Roger E. "Friends Missionary Prayer Band." In *Indigenous Missions of India*, edited by Roger E. Hedlund and F. Hrangkhuma, 100. Madras, India: Church Growth Research Centre, 1980.

———. "Indian Evangelical Mission (IEM)." In *Evangelical Dictionary of World Missions*, edited by A. Scott Moreau, 480. Baker Reference Library. Grand Rapids: Baker Books, 2000.

———. "Structures and Patterns for Third World Mission." In *Indigenous Missions of India*, edited by Roger E. Hedlund and F. Hrangkhuma, 21–37. Madras, India: Church Growth Research Centre, 1980.

Hibbert, Evelyn. *Training Missionaries: Principles and Possibilities*. Pasadena, CA: William Carey Library, 2016.

Hoke, Stephen and William D. Taylor. "Exposure to Other Cultures." In *Global Mission Handbook: A Guide for Crosscultural Service*, edited by Stephen Hoke and William D. Taylor, 107–8. Downers Grove, IL: InterVarsity, 2009.

———. "Hands-On Missionary Training." In *Global Mission Handbook: A Guide for Crosscultural Service*, edited by Stephen Hoke and William D. Taylor, 208–11. Downers Grove, IL: InterVarsity, 2009.

Hung, Vanessa. "Filial Piety and Missionary Calling." In *Worth Keeping: Global Perspectives on Best Practice in Missionary Retention*, edited by Rob Hay, 78–79. Globalization of Mission Series. Pasadena, CA: William Carey Library, 2007.

Ikels, Charlotte. "Introduction." In *Filial Piety: Practice and Discourse in Contemporary East Asia*, edited by Charlotte Ikels, 1–15. Stanford: Stanford University Press, 2004.

BIBLIOGRAPHY

Ingleby, Jonathan. "Preparation Time: What it Means." In *Worth Keeping: Global Perspectives on Best Practice in Missionary Retention*, edited by Rob Hay, 106–9. Globalization of Mission Series. Pasadena, CA: William Carey Library, 2007.

Interagency Language Roundtable. "Interagency Language Roundtable Language Skill Level Descriptions." https://www.govtilr.org/skills/ILRscale2.htm.

Johnson, Ian. *The Souls of China: The Return of Religion After Mao*. 1st ed. New York: Pantheon, 2017.

Ketelaar, Jaap. "Education: What it Means." In *Worth Keeping: Global Perspectives on Best Practice in Missionary Retention*, edited by Rob Hay, 57–61. Globalization of Mission Series. Pasadena, CA: William Carey Library, 2007.

———. "Spiritual Life." In *Worth Keeping: Global Perspectives on Best Practice in Missionary Retention*, edited by Rob Hay, 132–35. Globalization of Mission Series. Pasadena, CA: William Carey Library, 2007.

Kim, Dong-Hwa. "Ministry to the Elderly Parents of Missionaries." In *Worth Keeping: Global Perspectives on Best Practice in Missionary Retention*, edited by Rob Hay, 366–67. Globalization of Mission Series. Pasadena, CA: William Carey Library, 2007.

Kim, Hark Yoo. "The Retention Factors among Korean Missionaries to Japan." PhD diss., Trinity International University, 2001.

Kvale, Steinar, and Svend Brinkmann. *Interviews: Learning the Craft of Qualitative Research Interviewing*. Los Angeles: Sage, 2009.

Lai, Daniel W. L. "Filial Piety, Caregiving Appraisal, and Caregiving Burden." *Research on Aging* 32.2 (2010) 200–223.

Lambert, Tony. *China's Christian Millions*. 2nd ed. Oxford: Monarch, 2006.

Lane, Denis. *Tuning God's New Instruments: A Handbook for Missions from the Two-Thirds World*. Singapore: OMF, 1990.

Lee, David Tai-Woong. "Training Cross-Cultural Missionaries from the Asian Context: Lessons Learned from the Global Missionary Training Center." *Missiology* 36.1 (2008) 111–30.

Lee, Thomas. "A Mission China: An Analysis of its Ten Affecting Factors." In *Mission History of Asian Churches*, edited by Timothy K. Park, 21–44. Pasadena, CA: William Carey Library, 2010.

Lim, Valerie. "Finances: What it Means." In *Worth Keeping: Global Perspectives on Best Practice in Missionary Retention*, edited by Rob Hay, 340–42. Globalization of Mission Series. Pasadena, CA: William Carey Library, 2007.

Limpic, Ted. "Brazilian Missionaries: How Long are they Staying?" In *Too Valuable to Lose: Exploring the Causes and Cures of Missionary Attrition*, edited by William D. Taylor, 143–54. Globalization of Mission Series. Pasadena, CA: William Carey Library, 1997.

Lingenfelter, Sherwood G. "Intercultural Competency." In *Evangelical Dictionary of World Missions*, edited by A. Scott Moreau, 494–95. Baker Reference Library. Grand Rapids: Baker, 2000.

———. *Leading Cross-Culturally: Covenant Relationships for Effective Christian Leadership*. Grand Rapids: Baker, 2008.

Lingenfelter, Sherwood G., and Marvin K. Mayers. *Ministering Cross-Culturally: A Model for Effective Personal Relationships*. 3rd ed. Grand Rapids: Baker, 2016.

Loong, Titus. "Training Missionaries in Asia: Asian Cross-Cultural Training Institute." In *Internationalizing Missionary Training: A Global Perspective*, edited by William Taylor, 43–60. Grand Rapids: Baker, 1991.

Lustig, Myron W., and Jolene Koester. *Among US: Essays on Identity, Belonging, and Intercultural Competence.* 2nd ed. Boston: Pearson, 2006.

———. *Intercultural Competence: Interpersonal Communication across Cultures.* 7th ed. Upper Saddle River, NJ: Pearson Prentice Hall, 2013.

McKaughan, Paul. "Missionary Attrition: Defining the Problem." In *Too Valuable to Lose: Exploring the Causes and Cures of Missionary Attrition*, edited by William D. Taylor, 15–24. Globalization of Mission Series. Pasadena, CA: William Carey Library, 1997.

Meer, Antonia Leonora van der. "Personal Care of our Missionaries." In *Worth Keeping: Global Perspectives on Best Practice in Missionary Retention*, edited by Rob Hay, 153–55. Globalization of Mission Series. Pasadena, CA: William Carey Library, 2007.

Moon, Steve. *The Korean Missionary Movement: Dynamics and Trends, 1988–2013.* Pasadena, CA: William Carey Library, 2016.

———. "Missionary Attrition in Korea: Opinions of Agency Executives." In *Too Valuable to Lose: Exploring the Causes and Cures of Missionary Attrition*, edited by William D. Taylor, 129–42. Globalization of Mission Series. Pasadena, CA: William Carey Library, 1997.

Moreau, A. Scott, et al. *Effective Intercultural Communication: A Christian Perspective.* Grand Rapids: Baker, 2014.

Park, Timothy Kiho. "Korean Christian World Mission: the Missionary Movement of the Korean Church." In *Missions from the Majority World: Progress, Challenges, and Case Studies*, edited by Enoch Wan and Michael Pocock, 97–120. Pasadena, CA: William Carey Library, 2009.

———. "Missionary Movement of the Korean Church." In *Mission History of Asian Churches*, edited by Timothy K. Park, 153–73. Pasadena, CA: William Carey Library, 2010.

Peter's Wife. "Challenges of Single Women: Results of a Field Survey." In *Global Mission Handbook: A Guide for Crosscultural Service*, edited by Stephen Hoke and William D. Taylor, 174–76. Downers Grove, IL: InterVarsity, 2009.

Pirolo, Neil. "Raising the Standard for Missionary Care." In *Global Mission Handbook: A Guide for Crosscultural Service*, edited by Stephen Hoke and William D. Taylor, 171–74. Downers Grove, IL: InterVarsity, 2009.

Platt, Daryl. "A Call to Partnership in the Missionary Selection Process: Perspective of the Old Sending Countries." In *Too Valuable to Lose: Exploring the Causes and Cures of Missionary Attrition*, edited by William D. Taylor, 195–206. Globalization of Mission Series. Pasadena, CA: William Carey Library, 1997.

Rajendran, K. "The Emergence and Expansion of Indian Mission Movement from 1947–2009: A Study into the Successes and Failures." In *Mission History of Asian Churches*, edited by Timothy K. Park, 45–90. Pasadena, CA: William Carey Library, 2010.

Ro, David. "The Rising Missions Movement in China (the World's New Number 1 Economy) and How to Support It." https://www.lausanne.org/content/lga/2015-05/the-rising-missions-movement-in-china-the-worlds-new-number-1-economy-and-how-to-support-it.

Stark, Rodney, and Xiuhua Wang. *A Star in the East: The Rise of Christianity in China.* West Conshohocken, PA: Templeton, 2016.

Stirling, Allan D. "Missionary Attrition among Missionaries Serving in Asia and Europe." PhD diss., Trinity International University, 2002.

Taylor, William D. "Challenging the Missions Stakeholders: Conclusions and Implications." In *Too Valuable to Lose: Exploring the Causes and Cures of Missionary Attrition*, edited by William D. Taylor, 341–60. Globalization of Mission Series. Pasadena, CA: William Carey Library, 1997.

———. "Finances." In *Worth Keeping: Global Perspectives on Best Practice in Missionary Retention*, edited by Rob Hay, 339–40. Globalization of Mission Series. Pasadena, CA: William Carey Library, 2007.

———. "Introduction: Examining the Iceberg Called Attrition." In *Too Valuable to Lose: Exploring the Causes and Cures of Missionary Attrition*, edited by William D. Taylor, 3–14. Globalization of Mission Series. Pasadena, CA: William Carey Library, 1997.

———. "What about Missionary Attrition?" In *Global Mission Handbook: A Guide for Crosscultural Service*, edited by Stephen Hoke and William D. Taylor, 269–70. Downers Grove, IL: InterVarsity, 2009.

Turaki, Yusufu. "Evangelical Missiology from Africa: Strengths and Weaknesses." In *Global Missiology for the 21st Century: The Iguassu Dialogue*, edited by William D. Taylor, 271–83. Grand Rapids: Baker, 2000.

World Evangelical Alliance Missions Commission. "ReMAP II: Worldwide Missionary Retention Study and Best Practices." http://www.worldevangelicals.org/resources/rfiles/res3_96_link_1292358945.pdf.

Xi, Lian. *Redeemed by Fire: The Rise of Popular Christianity in Modern China*. New Haven: Yale University Press, 2010.

Yang, Fenggang. "Lost in the Market, Saved at McDonald's: Conversion to Christianity in Urban China." *Journal for the Scientific Study of Religion* 44.4 (2005) 423–41.

Yao, Kevin Xiyi. "The Chinese Church: The next Superpower in World Mission?" *Evangelical Missions Quarterly* 50.3 (2014) 296–302.

Yao, Xinzhong. *Religious Experience in Contemporary China*. Cardiff: University of Wales, 2007.

Zylstra, Sarah Eekhoff. "Made in China: The Next Mass Missionary Movement: Chinese Christians Plan to Send 20,000 Missionaries by 2030." *Christianity Today* 60.1 (2016) 20–21.

www.ingramcontent.com/pod-product-compliance
Lightning Source LLC
Chambersburg PA
CBHW050821160426
43192CB00010B/1844